How Oil Will Save the Earth

How established oil- and carbon-based products can accelerate the transition to greener materials, greener technologies, and a lower-waste world

By Abel Jiménez

Contents

Introduction - Why This Fight Matters

This book is written for mayors, utility executives, infrastructure leaders, contractors, engineers, climate practitioners, and high-performing professionals who are trying to lower the cost of modern life without pretending the physical world is simpler than it is.

Before we begin, I want to say this plainly: I am grateful. A big part of what I know came from leaders, operators, crews, and mentors who let me see their reality up close. They taught me where systems break, where costs hide, and how much trust matters when the work is public, dangerous, and expensive.

Costa Rica shaped how I think long before I worked in a startup. Its emphasis on renewables, stewardship, biodiversity, and doing a lot with little showed me that sustainability is not only an environmental posture. It is also a discipline of respect for limited resources.

Lean Six Sigma gave that instinct a working vocabulary. Lean taught me to look for waste embedded in process, handoffs, waiting, rework, and overdesign. Six Sigma taught me to see leakage, inconsistency, and weak controls as design problems, not as background noise.

A big part of my startup education then came from first-hand meetings with leaders and field workers from cities across Massachusetts and from companies across the East and West Coasts. I learned from Boston, Providence, Gloucester, Springfield Water Authority, the City of Worcester, Westfield, Cambridge, Middlesex, Framingham, Dedham, Chicopee, Boston Building Trades, National Testing System, high-density polyethylene (HDPE) manufacturers, National Grid, Consolidated Edison (Con Edison), Pacific Gas and Electric (PG&E), and contractors working beside state and federal institutions.

Some of those conversations were blunt in a way I have never forgotten. More than a few people told us that the market often rewards low implementation bids because maintenance and repairs can recover the lost margin later. That insight stayed with me because it explained why a money-saving idea can be technically right and still meet real resistance.

That is why I am not writing this as a manifesto against renewables or a sentimental defense of oil. I am writing it as a practical argument for lower-loss infrastructure, better materials, stronger verification, and a more honest conversation about total cost of install and total cost of ownership.

If my other work has been about how real change becomes durable inside organizations, this book is about how that same discipline applies to physical systems. In both cases, the hard part is not only strategy. It is trust, incentives, leadership, and turning a better idea into a standard people can actually live with.

That is where SolidMelt enters this story. I created SolidMelt because I believe we need a larger coalition around infrastructure, materials, and environmental sustainability: organizations, companies, institutions, governments, leaders, contractors, investors, operators, students, researchers, and passionate individuals willing to rethink how the world uses the carbon-based products already embedded in modern life. SolidMelt is not about asking society to abandon established systems overnight. It is about helping those systems waste less while greener materials and technologies mature, earn trust, scale manufacturing, and become available without forcing ordinary people to step outside the normal rhythm of life to live sustainably.

The core claim of this book is straightforward: I believe the next great breakthrough may not come from producing more of everything. It may come from wasting less of what already moves through the systems beneath modern life.

Important note: this book is not a product manual. It is a transition argument. It treats oil, petroleum-derived materials, and carbon-based products as the necessary bridge between today's infrastructure reality and tomorrow's lower-carbon systems. My claim is not that we should delay green innovation, but that we can accelerate its adoption by improving the established materials and systems already moving through the economy.

A new part of that coalition is the Global Ambassadors of Sustainability (GAoS), which describes itself as a nonprofit international network and think tank registered in Canada, with more than 13,000 members from 130 countries. GAoS frames its work around global leaders, collective action, and measurable sustainability impact, and its public materials emphasize sustainability practices, climate action, international partnerships, training, and green transformation. That mission fits this book because the transition I am describing is not only technical. It is educational, institutional, financial, and cultural.

GAoS and its related learning initiatives also reinforce one of the core arguments of this book: green transformation has to become practical, connected, and normal. A future built only on aspiration will not scale. A future built on training, leadership, procurement, practical bridge materials, and better use of existing carbon-based infrastructure can scale much faster.

The material adds a practical learning layer to that coalition. It captures sustainability not only as a technology question, but as a mindset question, a built-environment question, a workforce question, a finance question, and a water-resilience question. That is exactly why oil- and carbon-based bridge materials matter in the transition. They can help today's systems become cleaner, more durable, more measurable, and less wasteful while fully green materials continue to mature, scale, and earn market trust.

Why remote development became personal

I grew up in Costa Rica where rural distance was not theoretical. My father served as a minister, and some of my clearest memories are of traveling rough roads and muddy tracks to visit families in remote communities. There were places where water pressure could not be assumed, where humidity lived inside the walls, and where daily hygiene depended less on habit than on whether water, drainage, and electricity were available at that moment.

That experience stayed with me. Later in life, when illness and loss touched my own family, I stopped thinking of infrastructure as a neutral background condition. One of the women who helped teach me to read Spanish lived in a house where dampness and mold were not occasional nuisances but constant companions. By the time her illness was fully understood, it was too late. I cannot honestly reduce a life to one engineering variable, but I can say this with confidence: living conditions matter, indoor conditions matter, clean water matters, drainage matters, and the lack of basic services quietly shortens hope long before it appears in a budget line.

In the field, the theory became real

My confidence in this argument did not come from one white paper, one conference, or one good-sounding sustainability slogan. It came from the accumulated evidence of sitting with people who live these problems every day. During my startup years I learned directly from leaders and field workers in cities, towns, neighborhoods, and organizations. I heard the same lessons in conversations with National Testing System, HDPE manufacturers, major utilities such as National Grid, Con Edison, and PG&E, and with construction and contracting experts who work with state and federal institutions. They did not talk to me in abstract terms. They talked about what happens when an emergency repair crew gets called at midnight, when a trench stays open too long, when the police detail meter keeps running, when a pipe replacement turns into a week of traffic disruption, when a water outage closes businesses, and when a gas incident erases public trust faster than any public-relations team can rebuild it.

Those conversations also taught me something less comfortable. Many people in the system privately admitted that they survive on the inefficiencies that everybody publicly criticizes. Low implementation bids can win the job, but maintenance, emergency repair, mobilization, testing, and change orders can restore the margin later. That is not always fraud. Often it is simply the structure of the market: the first contract is lean because everyone assumes the lifecycle cost will be recovered somewhere else, later, and often by someone else. Cities absorb it in disrupted streets and overtime. Utilities absorb it in higher operating expense and rate cases. Residents absorb it in water bills, traffic, and service interruptions. The environment absorbs it in leakage, methane, and contaminated runoff.

The municipalities and utilities I learned from also showed me why this book cannot be written as a fantasy of instant adoption. The people who maintain old systems are not fools. Many of them are highly skilled, under pressure, and doing their best inside infrastructure that long predates them. But they are also operating inside budgets, procurement rules, labor agreements, inspection cultures, and business models that often reward reaction more than prevention. If I sound impatient at times in this book, it is because I have seen how much knowledge already exists in the field. We do not suffer only from not knowing. We suffer from failing to organize what we know into a standard that changes the economics of the job.

What the field kept teaching me about hidden cost

The deeper I got into startup work, the more I realized that the most important lessons were rarely delivered as theory. They came from operators, city engineers, utility crews, testers, contractors, and public officials who had already lived through the gap between what is specified and what actually happens in the street. I listened to people across the chain, from communities to town leaders, from town workers to city leaders, and from service providers to government officials. The same pattern appeared in different accents: the system looks manageable on paper until a weak point fails at the wrong time, in the wrong place, under the wrong weather, and then everyone discovers how much hidden cost had been sitting in the background all along.

That field reality shaped my passion much more than any single white paper could have. Lean and Six Sigma gave me a vocabulary for waste, variation, and process discipline. But the field gave me the emotional weight behind those words. Waste was not just extra motion or poor throughput. Waste was a ruptured main under a busy road. Waste was a crew waiting on broad testing when the uncertainty lived at one interface. Waste was a neighborhood disrupted because verification came too late. Waste was a public owner accepting low first cost and inheriting high lifecycle burden. That is why I care so much about savings in this book. I am not talking about clever accounting. I am talking about removing pain that people in the field have been forced to normalize.

Once I saw that clearly, I could not go back to discussing sustainability or infrastructure as if they were separate conversations. A system that leaks, corrodes, breaks in winter, or cannot be maintained cleanly is not only inefficient. It is environmentally careless, politically fragile, and socially expensive. That is the mindset I carry into every chapter that follows.

Chapter 1 - The Commodity Beneath Everything

"Reliable and affordable energy is the lifeblood of our economies." — *Ursula von der Leyen*

Oil became the world's master commodity because it solved more than one problem at once. It was fuel, chemistry, mobility, heat, logistics, and industrial power in a single resource. It could be stored, transported, refined into many products, and integrated into almost every layer of modern civilization.

That is why oil was never just about cars. It was about tractors, trucks, ships, planes, fertilizers, packaging, asphalt, plastics, industrial feedstocks, and supply chains. Once the world organized itself around oil, the price of oil stopped being the price of fuel alone. It became a shadow price on movement, manufacturing, and daily life.

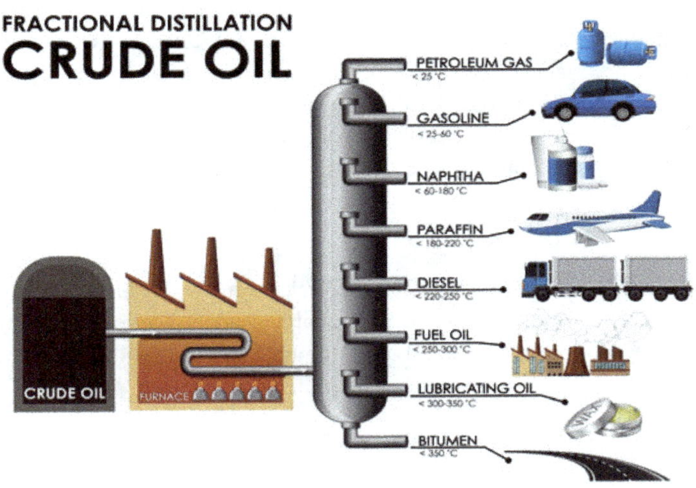

Even as electricity expands and energy systems diversify, oil remains deeply embedded in the physical economy. Aviation, petrochemical feedstocks, heavy transport, and long-lived industrial systems continue to depend on it. The future is not a clean handoff from one fuel to another. It is a messy industrial transition in which electrons do more work but molecules still matter.

This matters because the public argument about energy often treats oil as though it were simply an old fuel waiting to be replaced. That story is too small. Oil is also what the modern world is made from and what it moves through. Any serious argument about affordability must therefore look not only at how oil is produced, but also at how value is preserved - or lost - after production occurs.

That is where infrastructure enters the story. A civilization built on fluids lives or dies at the point of connection. If systems leak, corrode, fail, or demand costly workarounds, then oil's importance becomes even more economically intense. The future of oil is not only about wells and refineries. It is about whether the systems carrying value are designed to preserve value or lose it.

Deepening the Historical Lens

Figure 1.1. Modern life is illuminated by dense energy systems; the transition has to protect reliability while reducing waste.

What innovation ecosystems teach

When I was working inside the startup world, organizations like CleanTech Open, Greentown Labs, and the Massachusetts Clean Energy Center (MassCEC) made this lesson concrete. CleanTech Open describes itself as the world's largest cleantech accelerator and says it has worked with more than 2,100 startups, trained 4,000-plus entrepreneurs, and helped alumni raise more than $3 billion. Greentown Labs now says its community includes more than 200 climatetech startups, while MassCEC reports that since 2010 it has awarded roughly $990 million and helped attract about $3 billion in additional public and private funds. None of those institutions exists because invention is enough by itself. They exist because the real problem is translation: helping promising ideas cross the valley between technical credibility and market adoption.

When a commodity becomes a physical network

The more time I spent around utilities and infrastructure crews, the more obvious it became that oil became the master commodity not only because it powered engines, but because it quietly rewired the geometry of the modern world. Oil let us separate production from consumption by distance and still make the economics work. We could drill in one place, refine in another, manufacture in a third, and consume almost anywhere. That seems ordinary now because generations have grown up inside it, but the technical miracle was not only fuel density. It was the creation of a physical network that could move astonishing amounts of energy and material value through pipelines, ships, rail, trucks, and industrial process systems without collapsing under its own complexity.

Figure 1.2. Refineries turn hydrocarbons into fuels and feedstocks, placing oil at the center of both energy supply and material infrastructure.

That is why maps matter so much in this story. The network itself reveals the argument. The Pipeline and Hazardous Materials Safety Administration (PHMSA), the Bureau of Reclamation, the Massachusetts Water Resources Authority (MWRA), and state water agencies all tell variations of the same story: the systems that keep modern life functioning are sprawling, buried, interdependent, and expensive to interrupt. A pipeline map is really a dependency map. A water system map is really a public health map. A transmission map is really an affordability map. Once I began looking at the world that way, I stopped thinking of oil as merely a controversial fuel and started thinking of it as part of a wider infrastructural logic. It had become one of the underlying substances through which modern civilization organizes motion.

We can see that logic even in places where the fluid inside the pipe is not oil. MWRA's regional network exists to move and protect drinking water for millions of people and thousands of businesses. California's State Water Project exists to move water from one hydrologic reality to another. The Colorado River system exists as both a river and a constructed set of storage and conveyance decisions that support cities, farms, hydropower, and ecosystems across multiple states. In each case, once the network exists, the cost of failure rises far above the cost of the pipe itself. That is why I argue so strongly that the infrastructure layer belongs inside any serious conversation about oil, climate, and affordability. The commodity does not live in isolation. It lives in systems.

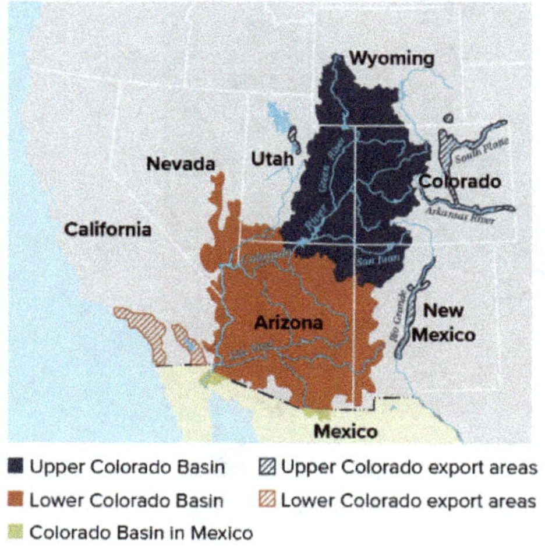

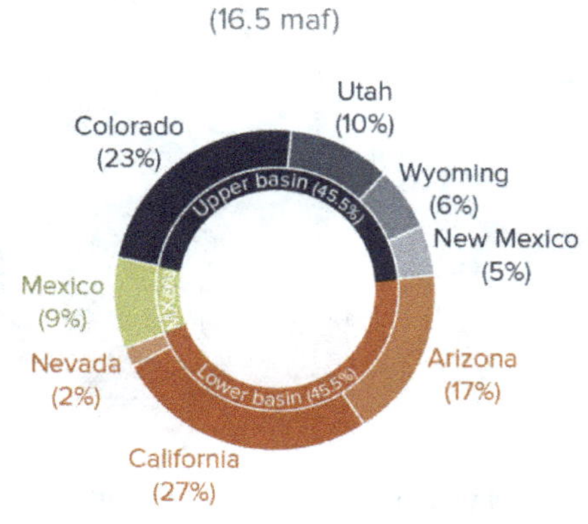

This is also why I am careful not to romanticize the past. When I say oil became the world's master commodity, I am not saying it became morally exempt. I am saying it became operationally foundational. That matters because foundational systems are harder to replace than people hope. They are not replaced by argument alone. They are replaced or reformed only when the substitute system can do the same civilizational work with equal or better reliability. That is a high bar. It is why the future will be built from a mix for a long time: more electricity, more renewables, more storage, more efficiency, but also better materials, better pipes, better leak detection, and better interfaces in the fluid-moving systems that remain.

When I look back on the municipalities and utilities that let me learn from them, I realize they were all teaching the same lesson in different accents. Commodity status is not just about extraction or price. It is about what society is willing to stop for. Cities stop for broken mains. Neighborhoods stop for gas emergencies. Traffic stops for trenches. Food systems stop when conveyance fails. Factories stop when process piping cannot be trusted. That is what it means for oil and its companion infrastructures to sit beneath everything. We do not need to worship that reality. But we do need to understand it if we want to change it.

Oil is also stored engineering

One reason oil became so dominant is that it does not only release energy when burned; it also becomes durable engineering when transformed into useful materials. That distinction matters to me because it changes the moral geometry of the conversation. A barrel refined into short-lived waste is one thing. Hydrocarbon molecules turned into long-lived, corrosion-resistant infrastructure that prevents larger losses are something else. HDPE sits exactly in that second category. It takes a hydrocarbon feedstock and turns it into a material platform for moving water, gas, chemicals, and industrial fluids with lower corrosion risk and lower handling burden than many legacy options.

Call to action: This week, trace one essential service in your world—from source to customer—and mark every place where value can leak out. When we can see the chain clearly, we can start protecting it.

Chapter 2 - Why the Price of Oil Becomes the Price of Life

"Energy security is right at the heart of this." — Keir Starmer

For me, this chapter is about translation. Commodity prices tell only part of the story. The larger burden shows up when weak systems turn normal volatility into repeated public cost, which is why affordability has to be discussed at the level of infrastructure as well as markets. I saw that link most concretely through water and methane infrastructure. MWRA serves millions of people and thousands of businesses through a wholesale regional network, while the public leak maps produced by Home Energy Efficiency Team (HEET) show what hidden infrastructure waste looks like when it becomes visible street by street. Together they reminded me that affordability is never only a commodity issue. It is also an integrity issue.

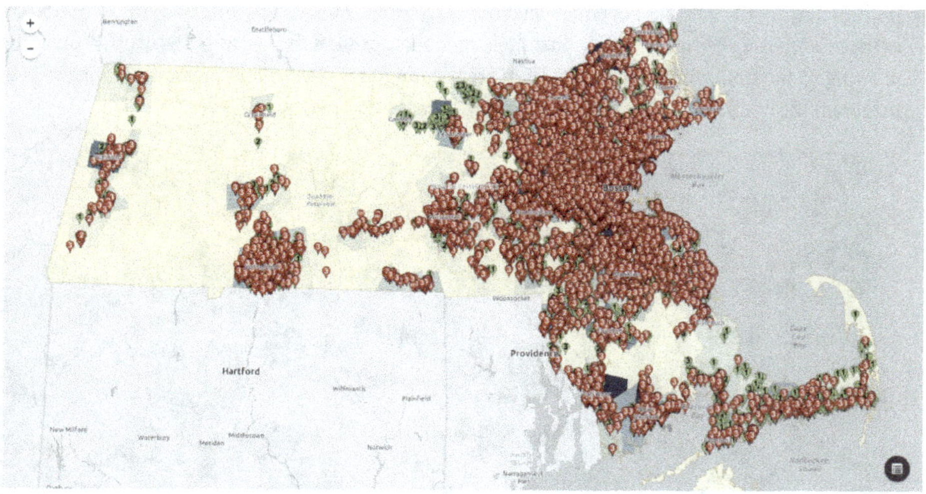

Most people notice oil when prices jump. Suddenly it is visible in gasoline, airline tickets, freight surcharges, food prices, utility bills, roadwork costs, and the price of anything that must be moved, built, heated, cooled, packaged, or maintained. Oil is different from most commodities because it does not stay in one sector. It passes through the economy like weather.

Food must be harvested, processed, packaged, and transported. Construction materials must be quarried, manufactured, shipped, and installed. Public works crews must move. Industrial equipment must be lubricated and maintained. Even when the final product is not made from petroleum, it usually travels through a petroleum-shaped world before it reaches the customer.

That is why oil becomes the price of life. Not because every product contains oil, but because nearly every system depends on motion, and motion has long depended on oil. When oil rises, freight rises; when freight rises, inventory costs rise; when inventory costs rise, retail prices follow. The same pressure shows up in municipal budgets, industrial bids, and household costs.

That is why lowering the cost of modern life requires more than better energy supply. It requires tighter systems. If the movement of water, gas, and oil can be made more reliable and less wasteful, then the hidden tax built into everyday prices begins to shrink.

Tracing the price signal

A price shock in oil does not stay confined to the fuel pump because the modern economy is not compartmentalized. Diesel prices alter trucking costs, which alter wholesale food costs, which alter retail margins, school lunch budgets, hospital procurement, and household spending patterns. Fuel costs affect municipal fleets, construction equipment, paving schedules, solid-waste operations, emergency services, and maintenance backlogs. Air travel, shipping, warehousing, and industrial inputs all absorb some part of the same signal. The reason the shock feels universal is that it is carried through multiple layers of motion and multiple layers of material dependence at the same time. This is why price volatility in oil so often produces a political reaction that feels much larger than the commodity itself. Voters are reacting to the multiplication effect. They are reacting to a system in which one change upstream moves through dozens of ordinary expenses downstream.

Figure 2.1. Transportation turns oil-price volatility into everyday cost as freight, commuting, food, retail, and public services move through fuel-dependent systems.

The hidden amplification mechanism is infrastructure friction. A tight and trustworthy system can absorb some price volatility with less public damage because fewer losses are embedded in delivery. A weak system cannot. It compounds the shock. Every leak, every repair mobilization, every repeated test, every emergency excavation, every service interruption, and every avoidable replacement adds cost where cost is already rising. So when the price of oil becomes the price of life, part of what people are really feeling is the interaction between commodity volatility and system inefficiency. That interaction is where infrastructure integrity stops being a technical concern and becomes a cost-of-living concern.

Lessons from building affordability

In my startup years, the water side of this problem became real through organizations like MWRA and the New England Water Innovation Network (NEWIN). MWRA says it provides wholesale water and sewer service to 3.1 million people and more than 5,500 businesses in 61 communities, while NEWIN says it helps municipalities, utilities, and tribes secure funding and technical capacity for safe, affordable, and resilient water systems. Those are not abstract examples. They show that affordability is inseparable from operating scale, maintenance discipline, and access to capital.

Organizations focused on building performance offer a useful analogy. WinnCompanies frames sustainability not simply as emission reduction, but as energy affordability and better operational decision making across real housing portfolios. That framing matters because it treats sustainability as a household-impact issue, not a symbolic aspiration. When building systems waste energy, tenants pay, operators pay, and public programs pay. The same is true in pipeline and distribution systems. When infrastructure loses product, loses pressure, or demands costly workarounds, somebody pays. The invoice may be delayed, hidden, or distributed across rates, rent, taxes, maintenance reserves, or capital plans, but it arrives all the same. That is why cost reduction at the system level is politically powerful. It addresses lived affordability rather than abstract efficiency.

The California Advanced Biofuels Alliance (CABA) points to the same principle from a different direction. Advanced biofuels matter not because they solve every part of the transition, but because they are deployable in sectors where the replacement cycle is slower, heavier, or operationally constrained. When an industry can lower emissions and improve resilience without waiting for a perfect future, it buys time, credibility, and public confidence. Pipeline innovation should be judged by that same standard of practical usefulness.

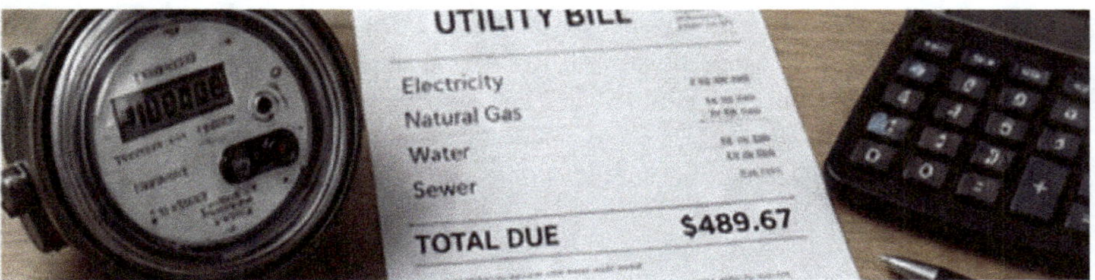

Figure 2.2. Utility bills make infrastructure friction visible, especially when energy, water, and waste costs rise together.

Why cost-of-life politics is changing

This is one reason affordability has become such a defining political issue. Citizens increasingly evaluate public narratives through the filter of lived systems: utility bills, maintenance disruptions, service reliability, housing cost, transportation cost, and resilience during extreme events. They do not care much whether a system sounds modern if it still feels punishing. That is why infrastructure arguments that stop at innovation language tend to stall. The public needs to see a line between operational improvement and human affordability. This chapter draws that line. It argues that lower-loss infrastructure is not a side benefit of modernization. It is one of the central ways modernization becomes believable to ordinary people. If the system wants public trust, it has to show that better design can make daily life less exposed to waste and less vulnerable to cascading costs.

Utility inflation is outrunning household resilience

The budget pressure is no longer theoretical. In February 2026, the Bureau of Labor Statistics reported overall consumer inflation at 2.4 percent, but water, sewer, and trash collection services were rising at 4.4 percent and water and sewerage maintenance was rising at 4.7 percent. That means core water-related costs were climbing at roughly 1.8 to 2.0 times the pace of broad inflation. For households already stretched by rent, insurance, and food, that spread matters.

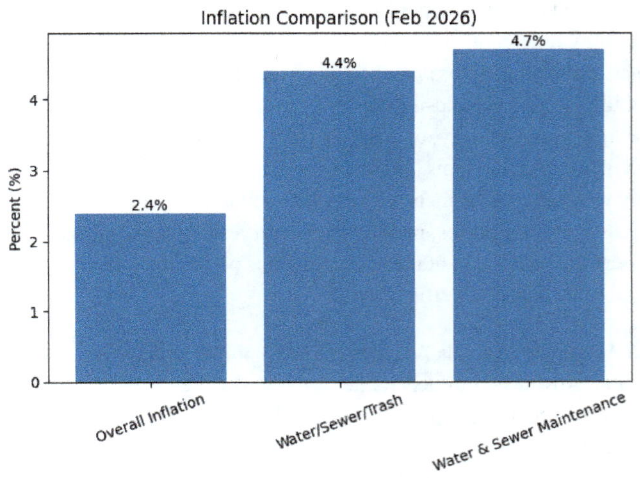

The same pattern shows up on the energy side. U.S. Energy Information Administration data show average residential electricity prices rising from 12.52 cents per kilowatthour in 2014 to 16.48 cents in 2024, a 31.6 percent increase. Residential natural gas prices rose from $10.78 per thousand cubic feet in 2020 to $14.50 in 2024, a 34.5 percent increase, even after easing from the 2023 peak. When electricity, gas, and water all move upward together, a city can claim inflation is moderating while families still feel that basic services are getting harder to hold onto.

Residential Energy Prices Rose Sharply Over the Last Decade

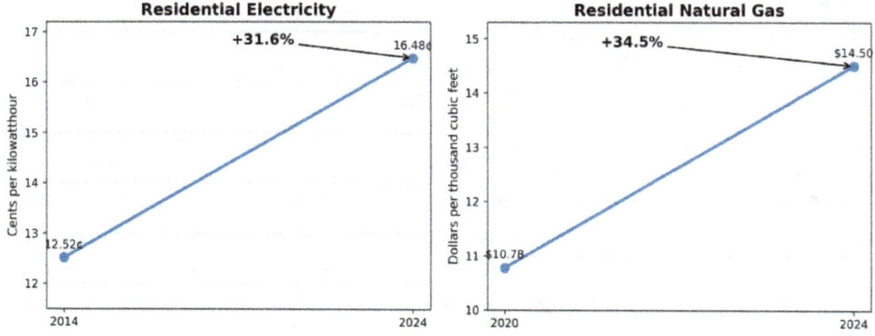

Source: U.S. Energy Information Administration data cited in text. Electricity: 2014-2024. Natural gas: 2020-2024.

The Department of Energy defines a high household energy burden as 6 percent or more of gross income. The Environmental Protection Agency uses 3 percent to 4.5 percent of household income as a water affordability range. Put those two official thresholds together and we are already in the neighborhood of 9 percent to 10.5 percent of gross income devoted just to home energy and water. That is the point where basic service begins to crowd out other necessities.

Cold weather turns hidden weaknesses into public invoices

One of the strongest examples of how infrastructure becomes the price of life shows up when winter hits an aging water system. The Washington Suburban Sanitary Commission, known publicly as WSSC Water, says bluntly that the chance of water main breaks jumps by about 60 percent in cold weather. The important detail is that the water main usually does not fail because it literally freezes. It fails because sudden temperature drops and freeze-thaw cycles shock the system, change soil pressures, and make already brittle pipe more vulnerable. In other words, winter does not create weakness from nothing. It exposes weakness that was already there. That is why I see cold-weather ruptures as a perfect case study for this chapter. They turn hidden asset condition into a very visible bill.

The cost of that bill is always larger than the repair crew line item. A large-diameter water main failure can force road closures, emergency excavation, traffic control, business disruption, overtime labor, pavement restoration, customer communications, and sometimes bottled water distribution or boil-water response. An empirical study of large-diameter main failures found that direct repair costs represented only about 35 percent of the overall consequence cost on average; property damage accounted for about 22 percent, and travel delays about 21 percent, with the balance made up by other indirect losses. That finding matters because it tells us something municipal budgets often hide: the utility does not pay the whole bill. Society pays the rest.

Waterbury gave us a recent, painful illustration of how quickly those indirect costs grow. Reporting in early 2026 described how the city's 2025 water crises drove roughly $33.7 million in repairs and system upgrades, including about $2.5 million tied to one major outage, $1.2 million tied to another, $230,000 for bottled water, and more than $146,000 in police overtime. Those numbers are not just about old pipe. They are about the compounding effect of not being able to isolate, monitor, and repair failures cleanly. They are about what happens when a system lacks the valves, segmentation, and trustworthy interfaces that let crews fix one problem without dragging half a city into the consequences.

What I hear in those failures is not simply that municipalities need more money. I hear that they need better economics. If we repair old systems using the same logic that made them brittle, we only postpone the bill. That is why SolidMelt matters in this chapter. When the development plan behind SolidMelt talks about saving pressure-testing time, progressively closing ditches, and reducing the open-trench period that requires detail officers and extended traffic controls, it is speaking directly to the cost structure of winter failures and urban emergency work. The savings are not abstract. They show up in shorter exposure windows, fewer lane closures, faster restoration, and less time paying for uncertainty in real estate that every city knows is expensive: the street.

I have seen how quickly a break changes the economics of a day. A break closes an intersection. A closed intersection delays commuters, buses, ambulances, deliveries, and contractors. Lost time becomes fuel burned, hours paid, appointments missed, restaurant traffic cut, and tempers shortened. The utility may book the repair cost under one line item, but residents feel the whole event as inflation. That is exactly why I say the price of oil becomes the price of life. Oil moves the trucks, powers the excavation equipment, shapes the price of asphalt and polymer materials, and also amplifies the social cost of every avoidable infrastructure failure.

The cold-weather lesson for infrastructure discipline

That matters even more as climate volatility increases. In some regions, we are getting colder bursts, hotter summers, more drought-driven soil movement, and more intense rain events in the same asset lifetime. The pipe that survives all of that will not be the pipe with the cheapest bid sheet. It will be the pipe system whose weakest points are best understood. That is why I keep coming back to total cost of install and total cost of ownership. The price of a connection is not its sticker price. The price of a connection is what the whole network must pay when that connection cannot be trusted under stress.

Utilities have been saying this for years in straightforward operational language. Milwaukee states that almost half of its annual breaks occur in December, January, and February, and that freeze-thaw cycles push pressure into the mains from the surrounding ground. WSSC Water has publicly warned that cold weather can raise break likelihood by roughly sixty percent when temperatures plunge fast enough to shock the pipe-soil system. Portland explains the same thing in different words: many breaks cluster in colder months, and the repair duration can range from a single shift to several days depending on access and damage complexity. What I take from those operational explanations is not just that winter is hard. It is that winter punishes networks that are already brittle.

Milwaukee's published average direct repair cost of about $2,400 per broken main is useful precisely because it is modest. It reminds me that the invoice paid by the utility is rarely the entire story. The more important number often sits outside the utility ledger: lane closures, detours, flooded basements, lost business traffic, police details, icing response, bottled water, and the reputational cost of a city that appears unable to keep its streets and service stable. Academic work on large-diameter failures makes this explicit. In one cost breakdown, direct repair represented only about a third of total loss, while property damage and travel delays consumed a striking share of the remainder. Society paid more than the utility did.

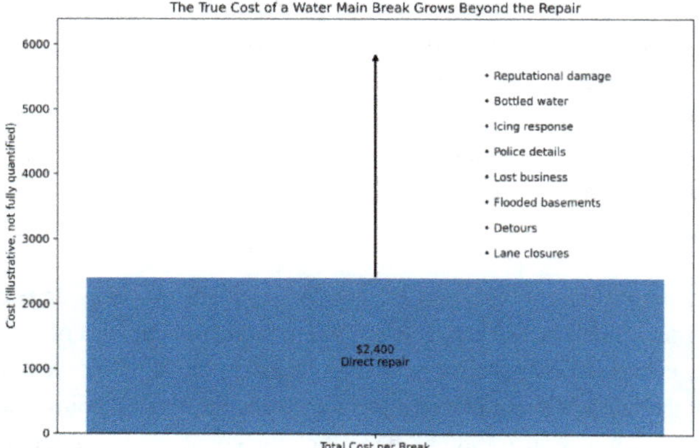

Waterbury, Connecticut, is an especially vivid recent case because the consequences were concentrated enough for the public to see the whole cost stack. Reporting on Waterbury's 2025 failures described not just repair spending but bottled water, police overtime, repeated outages, and the realization that missing valves and difficult isolation geometry can turn one pipe break into a citywide disruption. That is the kind of case I want procurement teams to study. Not because every city will face the same numbers, but because the pattern repeats: when systems cannot isolate, monitor, and restore efficiently, emergency work becomes an inflation machine.

This is exactly where the broader transition logic becomes useful. The strongest materials and infrastructure choices should be priced not only against conventional unit cost but against reduced pressure-testing time, progressive ditch closure, lower need for traffic-control overhead, and a broader total cost of ownership model. In winter, those savings become even more meaningful. Every hour shaved from open-trench time matters more. Every clean pass-fail verification matters more. Every avoided repeat excavation matters more. A city does not experience a winter break as a theoretical failure rate. It experiences it as exposure time. How long is the trench open? How long is the road closed? How many crews must remain onsite? How many downstream tasks are waiting on a repair that nobody can certify quickly enough?

That distinction matters for the future because climate volatility is not going away. Some places will live with less snow overall and sharper cold snaps when they do occur. Others will see more alternating freeze-thaw stress, wetter winters, heavier rainfall, and aging pipe exposed to more soil movement. In that world, the city that learns to reduce hidden break costs will feel more affordable than the city that continues budgeting as though direct repair were the whole problem.

If I were sitting with a mayor in a city that lives through repeated winter water-main failures, I would not begin with polymer chemistry. I would begin with the street. I would begin with overtime, detours, business complaints, school disruption, and the feeling residents get when a city that already feels expensive suddenly asks them to tolerate another burst pipe, another closure, another boil-water advisory, another week of emergency work. Mayors do not govern in the abstract. They govern inside accumulated frustration. That is where the case for SolidMelt begins.

I would say: your real problem is not only old pipe. Your real problem is that every break drags too many secondary costs behind it. The trench stays open too long. The repair geometry is awkward. The system cannot isolate gracefully. Traffic control becomes its own project. Bottled water, police details, restoration delays, and angry businesses all become part of a failure the public thinks of as a single event. But it is not a single event. It is a chain of costs. If you want to make the city feel more affordable, you have to start shortening that chain.

And I would be candid about resistance. Contractors who survive on change orders and repair work may not immediately celebrate a system that compresses uncertainty. Procurement teams trained to compare component prices may feel suspicious of lifecycle language. Some staff will worry that a more accountable interface means more demanding installation discipline. That is why demonstration matters. Pick the corridors where the public already understands the pain. Show the city what a lower-burden repair cycle looks like there. Savings become believable when they can be described in road hours, crew hours, and overtime avoided.

Finally, I would tell the mayor that success should be measured not only in direct repair spend but in recovered civic capacity. How many additional main segments can the city replace if it saves money on exposure and restoration? How much more resilient does the street network become if maintenance is better planned? How much more trust does the administration buy if infrastructure stops ambushing residents as often? Those are the right questions because they treat savings as capacity, not merely as accounting.

Why emergency water failures become inflation stories

I think we often miss how quickly infrastructure failures become everyday inflation because the chain has too many steps to feel dramatic. A water main ruptures during a freeze. Traffic detours start. Crews are mobilized. Police details may be needed. Businesses lose customer access. Restoration gets delayed. Asphalt repair gets added. Utility overtime expands. The next capital job gets pushed back because emergency money had to be spent first. None of those steps sounds like "inflation" in the abstract, but together they absolutely raise the cost of living.

That is why I treat water-main failures as economic signals rather than just maintenance events. If a city is constantly paying for emergency response, it has less room for planned modernization. If it has less room for planned modernization, it stays stuck with the assets most likely to fail again. That feedback loop is how hidden infrastructure weakness turns into a public affordability problem. We see the bill at the household level only after the system has already paid for it several times through labor, restoration, and delay.

Call to action: Choose one rate, bill, or repair pattern that people treat as normal and ask what infrastructure friction is hiding inside it. We change the cost of life by exposing the hidden costs first.

Chapter 3 - The New Politics of Energy

"You can't protect national security without delivering energy security." — Rishi Sunak

What I want to do in this chapter is make the politics practical. Energy debates now live inside resilience, trust, and public patience. Leaders are increasingly judged less by ideology than by whether the systems they oversee remain affordable and dependable under stress.

That is why coalitions matter. The Clean Energy Buyers Association (CEBA) advances the case for low-cost, reliable, carbon emissions-free electricity, and New England Clean Energy Connect (NECEC) shows how transmission debates quickly become debates about trust, affordability, and regional resilience. David Gardiner and Associates adds another lesson: infrastructure moves faster when communities can see tangible benefits and fair process, not just technical merit.

Energy is no longer only an environmental issue. It is a national security issue, an inflation issue, an industrial competitiveness issue, and a public trust issue. In a volatile world, governments are judged not only on ambition but on whether they can keep daily life affordable when global conditions turn unstable.

That shift changes the political meaning of infrastructure. A nation cannot credibly promise resilience while tolerating systems that leak, corrode, fail, and waste money. Public patience is thinner now. Utilities are under strain. Supply shocks are more visible. Voters experience energy not as a policy abstraction but as a monthly bill and a cost-of-living burden.

This is why the politics of energy is moving away from a narrow old-versus-new fuel debate and toward a harder question: which systems are affordable, dependable, repairable, and politically survivable? The next successful energy argument will not simply be the cleanest in theory. It will be the one that feels most trustworthy under pressure.

In that sense, the future standard is not only a better part. It is a better chain of trust.

Security, resilience, and trust

Heat resilience offers a useful parallel. Federal heat-resilience platforms such as Heat.gov and the National Integrated Heat Health Information System exist because climate stress becomes politically urgent when it affects lived safety, public services, and local decision making. These initiatives gather data, publish practical guidance, and help communities prepare for extreme heat because uncertainty is dangerous and expensive. Infrastructure policy is moving in the same direction. Leaders increasingly need systems that can be measured, justified, and trusted under pressure, not just systems that can be celebrated in strategy documents.

What coalitions teach about adoption

In the startup chapter of my career, I learned this lesson most vividly from projects and organizations like NECEC, CEBA, and David Gardiner and Associates. NECEC's public materials say the project would connect 1,200 MW of power into the New England grid and frame its case not only around emissions, but also around reliability, jobs, and lower consumer costs. CEBA, for its part, represents more than 375 members and tracks the procurement mechanisms that let buyers turn clean-energy ambition into financed projects. And David Gardiner and Associates' work on community benefits agreements argues that infrastructure earns staying power when transparency, accountability, and local benefits are made visible from the start.

Organizations working on building decarbonization have learned that a technically sound future still needs coalition building. The Building Decarbonization Coalition, for example, emphasizes policy alignment, market development, public engagement, and workforce development rather than treating electrification as a simple equipment swap. That is the right lesson for infrastructure more broadly. The future does not arrive because one technology is objectively better. It arrives when many stakeholders can see how the new standard fits their responsibilities, economics, and risk tolerance. That is especially true in sectors shaped by long asset lives and public consequence.

From ideology to operations

In that grammar, better connection integrity becomes politically meaningful. It helps convert abstract commitments into something durable and defensible. And in a century likely to be defined by compounding pressures, durability may be the most political quality a system can possess.

Figure 3.1. Energy politics becomes practical when reliability, industrial output, and public confidence all depend on the same physical systems.

Gas failures become political events in a hurry

If water main breaks are the affordability version of infrastructure failure, gas explosions are the trust version. They do not stay technical for long. They become televised, emotional, and political almost immediately because people understand viscerally what is at stake: fire, homes, injuries, lives, displacement, and the terrifying sense that the system beneath the street can suddenly turn against the neighborhood above it.

PHMSA's own research and reporting make clear that these incidents are not rare enough to dismiss as edge cases. A Department of Transportation research plan summarizing official incident data counted about 6,300 reported natural gas and hazardous liquid incidents from 2012 through 2021, including 280 serious incidents that resulted in 112 fatalities, 538 injuries, and more than $2 billion in property damage. Even where not every incident is an explosion, the official numbers are enough to make the point I care about here: failure at scale remains real, costly, and persistent.

In my view, that is the big lesson from San Bruno, East Harlem, and Merrimack Valley. Gas does not forgive weak governance. Once an operator loses the trust chain, the argument about energy security becomes harder to sustain. We can talk all day about affordability, supply, and heating demand, but if neighborhoods believe the distribution system is not rigorously controlled, every other argument starts from a hole.

Why earlier warning and cleaner isolation matter

When I think about the municipalities and utilities that taught me the most, I remember hearing the same practical concern in different words: crews can live with a hard job; what they hate is an uncertain job. Uncertainty creates work stoppages, repeated checks, extra trench time, more traffic control, more field supervision, and an argument afterward over what should have been obvious before the line went live. SolidMelt's promise in gas is not magic. It is discipline. It is the chance to buy certainty earlier, cheaper, and with less collateral damage.

Figure 3.2. Innovation requires trusted materials, skilled people, and disciplined testing before it can become part of public infrastructure.

And that is why gas disasters belong in this book. They make the stakes visible. They remind me that the cost of doubt is not a metaphor. It can be paid in burned homes, displaced families, shuttered blocks, and the kind of distrust that lasts long after the fire is out.

A gas utility lives under a different kind of pressure than a water department. The public expects water failures to be inconvenient. It expects gas failures to be terrifying. That difference changes everything. When I think about how to speak to a gas utility, I start with reputation and consequence before I start with procurement. The utility does not need to be told that incidents are expensive. It knows they are existential. What it needs is a credible path to shrinking the number of places where uncertainty can mature into a public event.

I would tell the utility that modern risk management is not just about responding faster. It is about shrinking the space in which a response becomes necessary. The more local certainty the operator can buy at the interface, the less it has to depend on downstream heroics. That matters for safety, but it also matters for organizational calm. Every utility executive knows what it is like to approve projects while worrying about what the next newspaper headline could make those projects look like in retrospect. Better interfaces reduce not just technical uncertainty but management anxiety.

Gas accidents change governance overnight

Another reason I frame energy politics through infrastructure is that gas accidents can change governance almost instantly. After a major explosion or overpressure event, the conversation is never only about the operator. It immediately becomes a conversation about records, inspection regimes, pressure management, emergency preparedness, penalties, procurement, and whether regulators trusted the wrong things for too long. That is why infrastructure failures are political accelerants. They compress years of ignored detail into one public reckoning.

I have seen how quickly the tone changes after a serious incident. What looked like back-office documentation yesterday becomes front-page evidence today. What looked like a manageable maintenance backlog becomes a legitimacy problem. What looked like an engineering detail becomes a governor's problem, a mayor's problem, a legislature's problem, and a ratepayer problem. In other words, system integrity is not just a technical attribute. It is a political stabilizer.

The politics of trust after failure

What strikes me most after major infrastructure failures is how quickly technical language becomes moral language. The public stops asking only whether the pipe was old or the pressure was wrong. People start asking whether the operator was honest, whether the regulator was awake, whether the contractor was supervised, whether the records were real, and whether the system cared about them before the incident happened. That shift matters because it shows that infrastructure trust is never merely mechanical. It is institutional.

Once trust has been damaged, the economic effects spread far beyond the asset itself. Emergency replacements accelerate. compliance costs rise. Insurance questions sharpen. Rate cases get harder. Public patience drops. Political leaders become more willing to intervene. In other words, one major failure can reprice an entire category of infrastructure risk. That is why I think risk reduction at interfaces deserves to be understood not only as an engineering benefit but as a trust-preservation strategy.

Call to action: In the next energy conversation you lead, insist on three questions at the same time: Is it affordable? Is it reliable? Can we prove it under stress? That discipline changes politics into stewardship.

Chapter 4 - Why Renewables Alone Are Not Enough

"The science compels climate action. So does the economics." — António Guterres

I am not making an anti-renewable argument here. I am making an implementation argument. If we want a cleaner future to stick, we have to respect the sectors, materials, and long-lived systems that still sit between intention and execution.

That is why I paid attention to groups like CABA and CEBA during my startup years. CABA's case for commercially available lower-carbon fuels in hard-to-electrify sectors reinforced a simple point for me: the transition has to work in the real world we have, not the ideal world we wish we already lived in. Infrastructure solutions gain traction when they reduce waste now while broader transitions continue to unfold.

The world absolutely needs more renewable power. Wind, solar, storage, electrification, and better grids are essential. But central is not the same thing as sufficient. A renewables-only theory of civilization is not yet a complete industrial plan.

The modern economy does not run on electricity alone. It also runs on molecules, materials, process heat, petrochemical feedstocks, aviation fuels, industrial supply chains, and long-lived infrastructure systems that move water, gas, chemicals, and oil. The energy transition is therefore not just a generation story; it is a materials story and a systems story.

Road transport can electrify faster than aviation. Buildings can be upgraded faster than heavy industry. But large parts of the world will continue relying on hydrocarbon-derived materials and fluid transport networks for years. The question is not whether renewables matter. It is whether the rest of the industrial story is being told honestly.

The strongest energy strategy is not renewable-only. It is anti-waste.

The incomplete transition story

I saw this incompleteness firsthand in startup conversations with groups like CABA, CEBA, and NECEC. CABA emphasizes that renewable diesel and biodiesel are commercially available now for heavy-duty trucking, emergency vehicles, farm equipment, and other uses where the transition is constrained by real-world operations. CEBA shows the buyer side of the same story: clean generation must be contractable and financeable. NECEC shows the transmission side: cleaner electricity still requires physical infrastructure and public consent to reach load.

Figure 4.1. Renewable generation is essential, but clean power still depends on grids, storage, materials, water systems, and delivery infrastructure.

A common mistake in transition discourse is to assume that if electricity can do more work, molecules therefore matter less. In reality, the system becomes more hybrid for a long time. Electricity expands, but heavy industry, aviation, shipping, long-lived pipe networks, feedstocks, and legacy building systems continue to require materials, thermal strategies, and transport infrastructures that cannot be wished away. This is not a counsel of despair; it is a design constraint. Good transition strategy starts with constraints. It asks what can be electrified rapidly, what can be electrified profitably, what requires complementary infrastructure, and what must be improved in place while the larger system evolves.

Evidence from buildings and housing

Building-sector examples are helpful because they show how hard real-world decarbonization can be even when the technology direction is clear. Research from the National Renewable Energy Laboratory (NREL) and policy guidance from states and federal programs repeatedly notes that multifamily and commercial building transitions involve cost, equipment, installation, financing, tenant impacts, and workforce challenges. Building electrification can improve safety, comfort, indoor air quality, and resilience, but it is rarely just a plug-and-play replacement. It requires planning and disciplined execution.

Clean-tech ecosystem lesson

Commercialization ecosystems taught me another essential truth: progress often comes through portfolios of practical solutions rather than one totalizing replacement. That is why I resist simple stories about abrupt transition. Durable change is usually layered, staged, and carried by many complementary tools at once.

Electrons alone do not solve the fluid-moving world

One of the reasons I resist one-solution narratives is that so much of the world I learned from is stubbornly physical. Buildings still need water. District systems still need heat exchange and circulation. Industry still needs process piping, cooling loops, chemical feedstocks, and reliable connections that can survive stress cycles. Agriculture still needs conveyance. Cities still need drainage, wastewater, reuse, and stormwater control. Even the clean-energy economy that I respect and want to grow is built on concrete, steel, polymers, insulation, cable, conduit, and a dense network of underground and above-ground distribution assets.

I believe the strongest version of the renewables argument becomes more persuasive when it acknowledges this. We need more renewable generation, more clean-power procurement, more efficiency, and more resilient buildings. We also need better ways to move water, wastewater, gas, recovered fuels, and industrial fluids through complex systems at lower cost. That is not a retreat from decarbonization. It is a completion of the decarbonization conversation. The cleaner grid will still fail politically if the water bills, gas safety crises, and infrastructure outages beneath it remain too expensive and too frequent.

Water scarcity makes the transition a pipe problem

The most honest way I know to say this is simple: the energy transition is also a water-management transition. Electrification needs transmission, storage, minerals, cooling, manufacturing, and construction. Agriculture needs reliable water even as snowpack becomes less reliable. Cities need more reuse, more interties, more pressure zones, and more resilience against both flood and drought. That means we are heading into an era where conveyance matters just as much as generation.

Figure 4.2. Climate resilience is also a pipe problem: water, wastewater, reuse, and industrial fluids must move through systems that waste less.

Research support: water reuse is part of climate resilience

- WRF frames reuse as a way for communities to diversify water supplies when drought, extreme weather, population shifts, and limited local sources make backup supplies critical.
- WateReuse describes reuse as a multi-benefit solution that can reduce energy use and carbon footprint versus other new supply options while strengthening drought and wildfire resilience.
- Implication for this book: cleaner energy still needs lower-loss water storage, conveyance, treatment, and reuse infrastructure.

Sources: Water Research Foundation Reuse topic; WateReuse Climate Policy Brief PDF.

California is the clearest example. The Department of Water Resources has been blunt that the Sierra Nevada snowpack is California's "frozen reservoir" and that it historically supplies about 30 percent of the state's water. When that snow comes later, melts earlier, or falls as rain instead of snow, the entire timing of the system changes. Reservoir operations change. River operations change. Groundwater recharge opportunities change. Urban and agricultural planning change. A warmer winter does not just create a climate anomaly; it creates an infrastructure problem.

That is why I pay so much attention to conveyance and storage. The California Department of Water Resources (DWR) has argued that Delta conveyance is essential because California will increasingly face more intense rain, less dependable snow, and wider swings between drought and flood. The agency has even said that if the project were operational during the 2025 water year, more than 956,000 acre-feet of water could have been captured so far. Whether one supports every element of that project or not, the message is bigger than California. Climate volatility is not reducing the need for infrastructure. It is increasing the need for smarter, more flexible infrastructure that can capture, move, store, isolate, and protect water when timing becomes the real crisis.

The Colorado River Basin tells the same story at continental scale. The Bureau of Reclamation describes the Colorado River as a system that provides water for more than 40 million people, supports 5.5 million acres of agriculture, fuels hydropower, and matters to Tribal nations, cities, farms, and industries across the American West. When a river system carrying that much value becomes stressed, the answer cannot be "just build more renewables" and stop there. We also have to talk about how water gets conveyed, conserved, recycled, reused, and protected from leakage all the way through the chain.

That is also why HDPE has such a compelling role. In saline, corrosive, or geologically dynamic settings, we need materials that do not ask us to spend the next forty years fighting the pipe. We need materials that resist corrosion, preserve hydraulic efficiency, tolerate movement better than brittle legacy systems, and reduce handling and installation burden when projects must be delivered under budget pressure. The Plastics Pipe Institute has long emphasized those advantages, and when I compare them with the costs cities face from repetitive failures, the case becomes hard to ignore.

So when I say renewables alone are not enough, I am not taking anything away from renewables. I am finishing the sentence. We need clean electricity and we need the fluid-moving systems that let societies survive climate volatility without wasting money and water every step of the way. In the coming decades, the places that adapt best will not be the places that only generate differently. They will be the places that move water, energy, and materials more intelligently than before.

Industrial heat, pipelines, and the honest middle ground

I also resist the false choice that says every honest climate strategy must either romanticize fossil fuels or pretend the hardest sectors will disappear quickly. Heavy industry, district energy, chemical production, aviation support systems, and long-distance freight all sit in the difficult middle ground. They need cleaner electricity, yes, but they also need molecules, thermal systems, and reliable fluid movement. Even the factories that manufacture clean-tech hardware depend on water supply, process piping, cooling loops, compressed gases, and waste-handling infrastructure.

Call to action: Pair one decarbonization goal with one delivery-system goal. If we want cleaner energy to last, we have to build the pipes, storage, testing, and maintenance discipline that can carry it.

Chapter 5 - Oil Used for Good

"The decisions we make regarding the energy sector will determine our success or failure."
— Luiz Inácio Lula da Silva

This is where the moral standard becomes clearer for me. I do not think oil deserves a free pass because it remains useful. I think it earns a public case only when oil-derived materials and systems reduce waste, harm, and avoidable loss.

Oil does not become good simply because it is still necessary. If oil is to have a serious moral defense in the twenty-first century, that defense must rest on stewardship rather than sentiment. Oil can only be defended where it helps reduce waste, prevent loss, improve resilience, and create systems that do less harm than the alternatives they replace.

That means the strongest case for oil is no longer 'burn more.' It is 'waste less.' Reducing methane leakage, improving pipeline integrity, using better materials, and building systems that preserve value rather than leak it away are the kinds of uses that make oil more defensible in a sustainability-conscious world.

That distinction is everything. Oil used carelessly invites criticism. Oil used to build tighter, safer, and more accountable infrastructure creates a different moral case. It says responsibility does not end at installation. The system must also prove it can protect what it carries.

In that sense, the ethical future of oil is not denial. It is accountability.

Defining good use more rigorously

When I was with a startup, groups like HEET, MWRA, and the regulatory logic behind the Clean Water Act made this moral test much more concrete for me. HEET's Massachusetts gas-leak work explains that utilities report leak locations annually and also notes that independent researchers often find 1.5 to 3 times as many leaks as utilities report. The Environmental Protection Agency's (EPA) summary of the Clean Water Act reminds us that discharges into U.S. waters are not a casual matter; the law exists precisely because loss and pollution do public harm. And utilities like MWRA demonstrate how much public value can sit inside a single large-scale water system.

To say oil can be used for good is to impose conditions, not to grant absolution. Good use means the hydrocarbon-derived material or system delivers measurable reductions in waste, harm, or instability compared with the alternatives realistically available in that context. It means the use supports resilience, preserves value, reduces leakage, or improves safety. It does not mean every existing oil use is defensible, and it does not mean the sector deserves a free pass because the modern world is historically dependent on it. This stricter definition is important because it keeps the argument honest. Without it, I would slide into mere defensiveness. With it, I can distinguish between uses that extend wasteful dependency and uses that help society manage an imperfect transition with greater discipline.

Examples of disciplined sustainability

WinnCompanies' sustainability work provides a useful non-pipeline example of what disciplined resource use looks like in practice. The emphasis is not merely on symbolic greenness, but on long-term portfolio performance, affordability, and responsible operating decisions. That mindset is exactly the one this chapter argues for. If a building owner can justify sustainability through lower energy use, healthier buildings, and more affordable operations, then an infrastructure operator should be able to justify better pipe systems through lower loss, lower maintenance, and stronger system trust. Good use is measurable use.

Figure 5.1. The strongest moral case for oil-derived materials appears where they protect water, ecosystems, and long-term public value.

Similarly, public heat-resilience efforts show how governments increasingly value practical interventions that reduce harm without waiting for ideal conditions. Heat.gov and the National Integrated Heat Health Information System (NIHHIS) exist because preparedness, information, and smarter local action save lives. The lesson transfers: public legitimacy grows when institutions use the tools they have to reduce real harm now, even as they work toward larger long-term change. A lower-loss pipe system fits that logic.

The Amazon as climate engine

The Amazon is often described as the lungs of the Earth. The metaphor is powerful, but the more precise scientific point is even more important: the Amazon is one of the planet's largest climate, carbon, and water-cycle regulators. The National Aeronautics and Space Administration (NASA) and allied researchers note that intact Amazon forests store enormous amounts of carbon, release vast amounts of moisture through evapotranspiration, and help generate the atmospheric "flying rivers" that distribute rainfall across South America. NASA has also highlighted that over the past fifty years roughly 17 percent of the Amazon's forests have been lost, while the remaining forest is much closer to becoming a net carbon source than many people realize.

That matters for me here because the destruction of forests functions like a slow cancer in the planetary body. It is not always dramatic in one single day. It spreads incrementally through clearing, fragmentation, fire, drought stress, and degraded water cycles. NASA Earth Observatory, the World Wildlife Fund (WWF), and Amazon conservation groups have all emphasized that deforestation weakens the forest's ability to recycle water, cool landscapes, protect biodiversity, and stabilize rainfall. A lung that is slowly scarred does not fail all at once; it loses capacity over time.

The forest argument also sharpens the moral case for HDPE. Used badly, hydrocarbons intensify environmental harm. Used well, hydrocarbon-derived materials can help prevent additional harm by making water conveyance, restoration projects, irrigation systems, wastewater systems, and lower-loss distribution networks more durable and affordable. The ethical line is clear. Oil is only defensible when it helps stop the bleeding rather than excuse it.

Leak elimination is climate work, not just maintenance work

I think one of the biggest public misunderstandings about sustainability is the assumption that climate action is mostly about new generation and cleaner fuels. Those things matter profoundly, but leak elimination is climate work too. HEET's mapping and methane work in Massachusetts helped me appreciate how tangible that truth is. A leak is not only a utility problem. It is an emissions problem, a safety problem, and a credibility problem. When independent researchers consistently find more leaks than utilities report, the issue is no longer merely technical. It becomes a challenge to the integrity of the whole system.

Figure 5.2. Leak prevention is climate work because it preserves product, reduces emissions, improves safety, and protects credibility.

The same logic applies to water loss. The Clean Water Act is not a pipe-replacement manual, but its emphasis on preserving the chemical, physical, and biological integrity of waters makes one thing obvious: the more we leak, overflow, cross-contaminate, and under-maintain, the more we shift cost downstream into rivers, aquifers, ecosystems, and human health. In a warming world, that cost compounds. Every gallon lost had to be pumped, treated, and financed before it disappeared. Every leak left unrepaired forces a system to do more work just to stand still.

This is where I think the "proper use of oil" argument becomes most defensible. Oil-derived materials such as HDPE can serve climate goals when they are used to reduce chronic system losses. A polymer that helps cut corrosion, leakage, and destructive excavation is not equivalent to careless combustion. It belongs in a different moral category because it prevents waste rather than causing more of it. That distinction matters to me because I do not want this book to sound like a blanket permission slip for the past. I want it to describe a more disciplined future in which hydrocarbons earn their place only where they reduce greater harm.

The Amazon makes that discipline feel even more urgent. NASA and WWF both stress that the Amazon is a critical climate regulator, a giant moisture recycler, and a major carbon store; NASA has noted that roughly 17 percent of the forest has been lost over the past 50 years. I understand why people call it the "lungs of the Earth," even though the metaphor is not biochemically exact. The deeper point is that we are damaging a planetary system that helps stabilize rainfall, heat, and biodiversity across regions far beyond the forest itself. If we continue to waste water, leak methane, and degrade the landscapes that regulate our climate, we are shrinking our margin of safety from multiple directions at once.

The Amazon is not a slogan; it is a system

When I call the Amazon one of the lungs of the Earth, I want to use the metaphor carefully. Forests are not giant oxygen factories in the simplistic sense that popular language sometimes suggests. They both produce and consume oxygen. But NASA and other scientific institutions keep reminding us that the Amazon is one of the planet's great climate engines. It stores immense amounts of carbon, it drives moisture transport across South America, and it helps regulate rainfall far beyond the forest itself. NASA has also noted that roughly 17 percent of the Amazon has been lost over the last half century. For me, that is the real point of the "lungs" language: we are talking about a living regulatory system that we have been cutting, burning, fragmenting, and drying out until its stabilizing function begins to weaken.

That matters to this book because I am not arguing for more careless oil use. I am arguing for a harder discipline: use hydrocarbon-derived materials where they reduce loss, extend asset life, and help us rebuild ecological resilience instead of undermining it. A corrosion-resistant HDPE water line that can help move reuse water, desalinated water, irrigation water, or restoration flows into degraded landscapes is not morally equivalent to a leaky system that wastes water, methane, labor, and capital. If we want future generations to inherit a livable climate, then we have to get better at separating useful use from destructive use.

I also think we underestimate the hydrologic consequences of deforestation because they are slower than explosions and harder to photograph than a rupture. When we remove large vegetation systems, we do not only lose shade and habitat. We lose evapotranspiration, local cooling, moisture recycling, soil stability, and the filtering capacity of roots and microbial systems. We also make downstream infrastructure work harder. Reservoirs silt more quickly. Flood peaks become more violent. Drought hits soils faster. Agricultural demand becomes more desperate. Then we spend public money trying to engineer our way around losses that a healthier landscape would have moderated for free.

That is why I see re-greening and pipe integrity as part of the same moral project. We need more trees, more wetland restoration, more vegetation, and better land management. But we also need the infrastructure to move water intelligently to the places where human settlement, agriculture, and restoration depend on it. If we are going to restore degraded land on the edges of deserts, protect food systems, or build greener urban corridors in overheated regions, then we need delivery systems that do not leak away value before it reaches the land that needs it.

The same logic applies to the Great Green Wall conversation and to other restoration efforts across arid and semi-arid regions. The lesson I take from those efforts is not that ecosystems can be engineered like factories. It is that nature and infrastructure have to stop being treated as opposing camps. A mature civilization will pair pipelines with revegetation, storage with soil health, and durable materials with landscape repair. We do not get to save the climate with rhetoric alone. We save it by reducing waste in steel, in concrete, in plastic, in water, in methane, and in the living systems that regulate heat and rain.

So when I say oil can be used for good, this is one of the tests I apply. Does the use help us keep more water in the system, more carbon in forests and soils, more reliability in agriculture, and more resilience in the landscapes that support human life? If the answer is yes, then we are moving toward stewardship. If the answer is no, then we are simply dressing up extraction in nicer language.

Call to action: Find one way hydrocarbons or hydrocarbon-derived materials can be used to prevent waste rather than excuse it. Saving product, water, and methane is not a side benefit; it is the moral test.

Chapter 6 - The Materials Migration

"We cannot manage this 21st century emergency with infrastructure from another age." —
António Guterres

In practice, materials decisions are rarely ideological. They are operational. Cities, utilities, and contractors migrate when an old material becomes too costly to defend across installation, maintenance, safety, and total cost of ownership.

Every industrial era leaves behind materials that once seemed permanent. Steel, copper, cast iron, and other legacy materials dominated because they fit the logic of their time: familiarity, standardization, and institutional comfort. But materials do not last because they are loved. They last because their total burden remains tolerable.

That burden is growing harder to defend in many legacy systems. Metal corrodes. Heavier materials demand more equipment and labor. More labor drives more cost. More cost delays replacement. Delayed replacement produces more emergency work, and emergency work is almost always the most expensive kind.

HDPE matters because it changes several variables at once. It can reduce corrosion risk, ease handling, lower installation costs, preserve flow performance, and reduce long-term maintenance burdens in the applications where it is well suited. It offers a lower-friction operating model rather than simply a different material.

Why materials change slowly

In startup work, I repeatedly saw that material transitions are slowed less by physics than by institutional muscle memory. Water organizations like MWRA and capacity-builders like NEWIN helped me appreciate how much installed systems, procurement habits, and funding pathways shape what can realistically be adopted. A better material must fit not just an engineering specification but a maintenance budget, a capital plan, a contractor base, and a regulator's comfort zone.

Materials migrations are often misread because observers focus on physical properties while underestimating institutional inertia. Engineers, contractors, inspectors, insurers, utilities, and procurement teams do not adopt a new material only because it is lighter or more corrosion resistant. They adopt it when the broader package of handling, installation, lifecycle cost, supply chain familiarity, field training, and risk perception shifts enough to outweigh the cultural security of the old material. This is why steel and copper can remain entrenched even where their full lifecycle burden is increasingly difficult to defend. The installed knowledge around them remains powerful.

HDPE therefore has to be understood not just as a better material in many use cases, but as the centerpiece of a change-management problem. The migration succeeds when the market stops asking only whether HDPE can perform and starts recognizing that the older material system may no longer be economically reasonable once corrosion, weight, labor intensity, maintenance, and repeated failure are honestly costed.

Miami is what the material argument looks like in the real world

If I had to choose one place to explain why material choice has become strategic rather than merely technical, Miami would be near the top of the list. The City of Miami, for its part, is explicit about what sea-level rise means locally: higher groundwater, less natural drainage capacity, more king-tide flooding, contamination risk for aquifers and agricultural soils, and greater stress on stormwater and drinking-water systems. Miami-Dade's own environmental materials add another layer by explaining how septic contamination can move through a porous aquifer that also underlies the region's drinking water supply.

Figure 6.1. Coastal environments make material choice strategic by exposing corrosion, handling burden, and lifecycle cost in plain sight.

The National Oceanic and Atmospheric Administration's (NOAA) work on southeast Florida septic hotspots makes the urgency even more concrete. Groundwater in the region is never far from the surface, and high water tables plus sea-level rise can infiltrate septic systems and cause them to leach untreated waste. NOAA notes Miami-Dade estimates that 64 percent of its septic systems are periodically compromised by groundwater infiltration. That is exactly the type of mixed-system vulnerability that persuades me the future will need a great deal more pipe replacement and sewer conversion, not less. And when that buildout happens, material choice will determine whether we build a resilient network or just an expensive one.

Miami is one of the most important water examples in the country because it forces us to see how multiple vulnerabilities can pile onto the same system at once. Saltwater intrusion is not a distant concept there. The Biscayne aquifer is shallow, porous, heavily used, and exposed to both coastal pressure and inland contamination pathways. USGS has documented the inland movement of the saltwater front in parts of Miami-Dade. The county itself repeatedly emphasizes that the aquifer is highly vulnerable because of its porous limestone geology. When streets flood during king tides and groundwater rises from below, that is not only a nuisance story. It is a systems-integrity story.

The wastewater side makes the case even sharper. Miami-Dade has had well over one hundred thousand septic systems, many in areas vulnerable to groundwater intrusion. County materials and federal coastal-science work both note that a large share of these systems are periodically compromised when groundwater rises. Once that happens, the tidy policy distinction between stormwater, wastewater, and drinking-water protection starts to dissolve in the real world. Canals, shallow groundwater, septic effluent, and drinking-water protection all interact inside the same porous landscape. That is why Miami matters so much to a book like this one. It shows us that contamination risk is increasingly about interfaces between systems, not just isolated assets.

In that environment, HDPE becomes more compelling because corrosion is the wrong fight to keep fighting. Metal systems in saline or high-groundwater conditions force owners to spend years managing the material's environmental disadvantages. HDPE starts from a different premise. It is chemically resistant, non-corrosive, and widely used in marine and highly aggressive environments precisely because the material is not constantly at war with the setting in which it operates. Add heat-fused continuity and the system begins to behave more like one restrained structure rather than a chain of vulnerable mechanical transitions.

Miami also reminds me that the water argument can never be limited to leaks alone. In a porous aquifer, contamination can travel through what the system allows to connect. If wastewater pathways, saline intrusion, stormwater pressure, and drinking-water infrastructure are all tightening around the same urban footprint, then every improvement in pipe integrity does double work. It reduces product loss and it reduces the chances that a compromised corridor becomes a contamination corridor. That is why I reject the old idea that municipal water should be discussed only as a utility topic. In coastal cities it is a public-health, land-use, climate-adaptation, and real-estate topic at the same time.

SolidMelt's cost argument belongs here too. In places like Miami, the total cost of install and total cost of ownership cannot be reduced to commodity pipe price. The relevant costs include groundwater management, access complexity, corrosion burden, restoration, future inspection, and the cost of failure in high-value urban land. When an internal plan says we should price against open-trench time, maintenance burden, and lifetime economics, that is not just a sales tactic. It is a better way to describe reality in the hardest environments.

Stormwater cities show why non-porous, fused water systems matter

New York gives me one of the clearest examples of what happens when climate, transit, sewage, and drinking-water risk start colliding in the same urban footprint. The Metropolitan Transportation Authority (MTA) says it pumps roughly 14 million gallons of water out of the subway system on a typical day, yet extreme storms still overwhelm that infrastructure. During Superstorm Sandy, corrosive floodwater damaged all 11 of the system's under-river tunnels, and the F line's Rutgers Tube alone took in about 1.5 million gallons of saltwater. At the surface, the New York City Department of Environmental Protection (DEP) says climate change is bringing more sudden and powerful storms, and in coastal areas high tide combined with storm surge can push tidal water back into the sewer system, forcing overflows through manholes, catch basins, and basement connections. DEP also notes that about 60 percent of New York City is served by combined sewers, meaning heavy storms can mix runoff and sewage and discharge that mixture directly into local waterways.

Boston may express the problem differently, but it is living inside the same logic. Boston's climate-resilience work says stronger storms and sea-level rise are already threatening low-lying infrastructure and that about one-sixth of the city sits on fill that is especially vulnerable to flood pathways. City materials tied to Climate Ready Boston are explicit that some T stations are already vulnerable in extreme events, including the John F. Kennedy/University of Massachusetts station (JFK/UMass), Sullivan Square, many Blue Line stations in East Boston, and vulnerable Silver Line stations on the South Boston waterfront. Boston's sewer agencies are just as clear about the water-quality side of storm stress: in large wet-weather events, combined sewer systems can be overwhelmed, causing rainwater to mix with wastewater and discharge to nearby waters, and public-health alerts warn people to avoid contact after those events because of bacteria and other pollutants.

I have noticed that material arguments become clearer when we stop treating 'best option' as a universal claim and instead ask a tougher question: best option for what environment, what failure mode, and what maintenance regime? That is the right way to think about HDPE. It is not best because it is fashionable. It is best in many of the environments we now care most about because its material properties line up with the stresses those environments impose.

If I were speaking to a coastal county like Miami-Dade or any county moving in that direction, I would say the worst mistake is to keep treating each water problem as if it belongs in its own silo. Saltwater intrusion is not isolated from septic conversion. Septic conversion is not isolated from street flooding. Street flooding is not isolated from groundwater rise. Groundwater rise is not isolated from drinking-water vulnerability. Once the aquifer, the streets, and the wastewater system begin pushing on one another, patchwork becomes its own liability.

That is why coastal resilience requires a harder kind of prioritization. Counties need to choose materials and interfaces that reduce future vulnerability while they are already spending money to adapt. If we are going to dig up roads, convert districts to sewer, upgrade pump stations, or relocate vulnerable corridors, we should stop pretending the cheapest component is automatically the most responsible choice. In coastal conditions, the future bill for corrosion, access difficulty, restoration, and contamination risk arrives quickly. The county pays it whether the original procurement model recognized it or not.

Why flexibility, segmentation, and fused integrity matter on coasts

Coastal systems are rarely dealing with one problem at a time. They are dealing with salt, standing water, traffic, settlement, storm surge, groundwater rise, and the political sensitivity of repeated street flooding. That complexity is why I put so much emphasis on flexibility and segmentation. Flexible pipe helps survive ground movement. Fused integrity helps limit leak paths. Better segmentation helps isolate failures without dragging an entire district into the repair. If we are honest about the future coastal cities face, then we should be honest that conventional corrodible materials and vague connection assurance are a poor fit for that future. Miami is not a special case anymore. It is an early warning.

Coastal adaptation is a materials decision

What I keep seeing in coastal examples is that climate adaptation is not only a drainage or seawall issue. It is a materials issue. Saltwater intrusion, rising groundwater, nuisance flooding, and repeated wetting-drying cycles punish traditional systems mercilessly. If we respond to those conditions with materials that corrode easily, crack under movement, or demand expensive protective measures just to survive their environment, then we are building high maintenance into the future from the very beginning.

Why HDPE wins when chemistry turns hostile

I come back again and again to one simple engineering question: what is the environment asking the material to survive? In a benign setting, a lot of materials can look adequate on day one. In a harsh setting - salinity, variable groundwater, corrosive soils, repetitive wet-dry cycles, settlement, freeze-thaw, or chemical exposure - adequacy disappears quickly. The life of the asset becomes a maintenance contest. That is where HDPE begins to separate itself.

Figure 6.2. Fused, corrosion-resistant systems can shift the economics of trust when chemistry, water, and soil conditions turn hostile.

The case is not that HDPE is magical. The case is that it eliminates several chronic failure drivers at once. It does not corrode the way metal systems corrode. It handles many chemical environments better than older alternatives. It stays lighter in handling and often simpler in installation. It keeps a smoother bore over time. And when properly joined, it helps create a fused system logic instead of a network of dissimilar mechanical vulnerabilities. In places where climate stress is increasing and service interruptions are politically costly, that bundle of advantages matters far more than the old instinctive preference for "heavier equals stronger."

What medicine teaches me about purity and material trust

When I want to explain why HDPE deserves more respect in water service, I sometimes borrow a comparison from medicine because it cuts through marketing language fast. Polyethylene is not just a construction polymer. Peer-reviewed medical literature describes porous high-density polyethylene as a biocompatible, durable, nonresorbable implant material used in craniofacial, orbital, ear, and skull reconstruction. A recent systematic review of high-density porous polyethylene cranioplasty reported favorable outcomes and high rates of contour improvement and patient satisfaction, and earlier reconstructive work found polyethylene implants well tolerated as replacements for native cartilage in auricular reconstruction. I do not use those examples to blur the line between surgery and civil engineering. I use them because they show how seriously the world already treats the stability, cleanliness, and long-term trustworthiness of this family of materials when the stakes are intimate and unforgiving.

There is an important nuance here. The medical form is intentionally porous so living tissue can grow into it. The potable-water form I am defending is the opposite at the fluid boundary: solid-wall, smooth, and non-porous where the water travels. But the common lesson is material trust. In both settings, polyethylene is valued because it resists corrosion, does not rust, and is expected to remain chemically stable under demanding conditions. In the human body that means minimizing adverse reaction while maintaining structure. In a drinking-water line, it means protecting the contents from corrosion-driven contamination, metal release, taste change, and avoidable intrusion.

The medical analogy also sharpens the cost argument. If specific forms of polyethylene are already trusted in the human body when designed and implanted correctly, why would we keep treating them as second-rate in the much rougher world of floodwater, salt exposure, repeated excavation, and drinking-water movement? The better question is not why fusing costs a little more up front. The better question is why we would gamble on lower first cost when the penalty for contamination, corrosion, and repeated repair is so much higher over the life of the system.

This is why I think the "best option" language has to be understood correctly. HDPE is not best because it is fashionable. It is best in many of these applications because the environment is telling us what the old system can no longer do affordably. If the ground is salty, if the water table is changing, if rehabilitation windows are tight, and if owners need long asset life with lower maintenance burden, then choosing a corrosion-resistant, flexible, fused polymer system is not ideology. It is adaptation.

Call to action: Review one asset class in your organization through lifecycle cost instead of first cost alone. The best material decision is usually the one that removes the most future repair, corrosion, and uncertainty.

Chapter 7 - Infrastructure Is the Battlefield

"Big systems fail at small interfaces." — Abel Jiménez

A system can have excellent material, sound engineering, and competent crews, yet still be undermined by uncertainty at the interface. That uncertainty is expensive. It drives broad testing, extra supervision, callbacks, excavation, service interruption, and the lingering fear that a buried weakness will return later at full price.

Why interfaces dominate risk

My startup experience with HEET and water-infrastructure stakeholders made this painfully visible. HEET's maps turn hidden methane loss into something spatial and public; its Massachusetts leak map notes that the locations are only a snapshot and that independent researchers often detect more leaks than utility reports alone show. The Clean Water Act provides the analogous lesson on the water side: once a leak or failure threatens water quality, the issue stops being local workmanship and becomes public policy.

Figure 7.1. Infrastructure risk often concentrates at buried interfaces, where small uncertainties can become large public costs.

Research support: methane visibility is an infrastructure strategy

- EDF reports that more than 100 technologies are commercially available to find and fix emissions across more than 3 million miles of pipeline.
- EDF also estimates U.S. onshore gas pipeline leakage at 3.75 to 8 times the EPA greenhouse-gas inventory estimate, making better detection and faster repair economically and environmentally significant.
- Implication for this book: proof at the interface is not a luxury; it is a governance, safety, and climate tool.

Sources: EDF pipeline methane leaks report and EDF pipeline-emission rules release.

From assumption to visible proof

Innovation ecosystems often fail because they underestimate how much of industry still runs on assumption disguised as confidence. Customer discovery and field validation matter because markets do not adopt new standards merely because they are elegant. They adopt them when someone proves they solve a painful, expensive, and persistent problem.

Figure 7.2. Local proof at the connection point reduces uncertainty before the trench is closed and the public inherits the risk.

Three failures that show why interfaces matter

San Bruno offers a second lesson. In 2010, a natural gas transmission pipeline ruptured and burned in a residential neighborhood in California. Eight people died, dozens were injured, homes were destroyed, and the event became a national warning about records, materials, welding, integrity management, and the price of assuming a buried system is fine because the paperwork says it should be. Transmission and distribution are different worlds, but the shared lesson is that buried uncertainty does not stay buried forever. Eventually it converts into human harm.

East Harlem offers a third lesson. The NTSB's investigation into the 2014 building explosion and fire in New York traced the event to a gas leak and a failed plastic service tee connection. Eight people were killed. The detail that stays with me is not just the tragedy itself. It is the reminder that even when polymer pipe is part of the answer, the interface still determines whether the system behaves like an asset or a threat. Good material does not rescue a weak connection culture.

For me, that is the battlefield. Not the heroic narrative of the pipeline, but the humble point where buried trust is either earned or betrayed. Every major incident that passed through an interface makes that truth harder to deny.

Interfaces are where old and new systems meet

Call to action: Identify the weakest interface in your current system and make it visible to the people who fund, build, and maintain it. We stop paying for invisible risk when we stop treating it as invisible.

Chapter 8 - Carbon-Based Transition Materials as the Bridge

"Restore the balance between growth and sustainability." — Luiz Inácio Lula da Silva

This chapter reframes the argument away from proprietary product design and back toward the broader transition challenge. Oil- and carbon-based products are already embedded in the systems that move water, energy, chemicals, food, medicine, and building materials. The practical question is how to improve those products so they leak less, last longer, waste less energy, and make room for greener materials to scale with lower risk.

I do not see oil-based products as the final destination. I see them as the necessary transition. A responsible transition does not demand that society throw away every established material overnight. It asks us to modify and upgrade today's petroleum-based materials so they reduce corrosion, reduce emissions, preserve purity, cut maintenance burdens, and lower total cost while lower-carbon alternatives become more trusted, easier to manufacture, and more widely available.

That is why I argue for disciplined improvement rather than dramatic rupture. If we improve the carbon-based products already serving industry and public infrastructure, we can create environmental savings now: less waste, fewer emergency repairs, less product loss, lower embodied replacement cost, and better operating conditions for the next generation of green technologies. In that sense, better petroleum-derived materials can function as an accelerator for decarbonization rather than an excuse to delay it.

This chapter is where the argument becomes practical. A product only matters if it changes the operating reality for the people who install, test, maintain, regulate, insure, and ultimately pay for the system.

From product to category

When I was in startup life, I learned how categories are actually built through incubators, accelerators, public agencies, and early customer networks. The strongest ecosystems do not just help founders refine pitches; they help markets understand why a technology deserves new language, new partnerships, and new procurement expectations.

Why standards beat novelty

Figure 8.1. Bridge materials matter when they reduce leakage and lifecycle burden inside the systems society already depends on.

From sticker price to total cost of ownership

The SolidMelt development plan gives us one of the clearest commercial truths in this entire story: the most important number is not the first number in the bid tab. The plan explicitly says that the product should be priced and sold against total cost of ownership, not only against the cheapest immediate unit price. It goes even further by naming the near-term savings that matter in real field work: reduced pressure-testing time, the ability to progressively close ditches so follow-on work can begin sooner, reduced requirement for police details while open trenches remain, simpler maintenance, and the ability to build value around lifecycle benefits instead of unit cost alone.

When I say SolidMelt can save money, I do not mean it in a vague inspirational sense. I mean it can potentially save testing cost, transportation disruption cost, maintenance cost, and the total cost of install by reducing the time and scope of the most expensive activities. It can save total cost of ownership by lowering the price of doubt over the life of the asset. And that is not just a utility accounting point. It is a civic point. The owner of infrastructure is always ultimately the public, even when the invoice is routed through a utility or contractor first.

Why lower transportation and restoration burden matter so much

I want to be careful in the technical case for HDPE because the strongest argument is a disciplined one. HDPE is not magic and should not be sold that way. It is not automatically the right answer for every diameter, fluid, temperature, or installation environment. But within its pressure and application envelope, it solves a bundle of problems that older materials often solve only expensively. That is why I call it strategic rather than merely cheap.

Add weight and handling. Lighter material affects transportation cost, jobsite safety, and labor burden. It changes what equipment is required, how fast sections can be moved, and how quickly a crew can stage work. In congested urban environments, that matters enormously because every extra truck movement and every extra hour of setup translates into public disruption. The original SolidMelt plan repeatedly ties product value to exactly these field realities: lower material, shipping, and storing costs; easier handling; reduced pressure-testing time; and faster progress through the work zone.

Add resilience to movement. Flexible materials handle ground settlement, minor seismic activity, temperature change, and some forms of dynamic loading differently from brittle legacy materials. That is one reason HDPE has become attractive in coastal, seismic, or otherwise unstable environments. The more our cities and landscapes are stressed by flood, drought, subsidence, or heat, the more valuable flexibility becomes. A pipe system that tolerates movement can save an owner multiple future repairs that never show up in the original unit price comparison.

Why melting is the price of purity

I would rather pay once for controlled melting than pay repeatedly for contamination risk, leakage, repeat excavation, boil-water orders, and the public-health costs of letting dirty floodwater, saline groundwater, or sewage-laden runoff find their way through old weaknesses. When I frame it that way, the upfront fusion premium stops looking like a nuisance and starts looking like what it really is: a disciplined investment in cleaner transport.

Figure 8.2. Cleaner joints and controlled installation can lower contamination risk, shorten trench exposure, and improve total ownership cost.

The reason I keep returning to the word save is that it is the most underestimated strategic word in infrastructure. People hear savings and assume modesty. I hear sequence. A city that saves money on trench exposure, testing overhead, repeat excavation, and avoidable maintenance buys itself the ability to do something else with that money. It can replace more brittle pipe. It can fund another resilience project. It can convert septic neighborhoods to sewer. It can add storage, reuse, or conveyance. It can build the next layer instead of spending every dollar compensating for the weaknesses of the last one.

That is also why public case studies matter in this book. They turn an engineering claim into a lived claim. A gas disaster shows what interface failure can do at neighborhood scale. A winter water break shows what aging assets do to public budgets. A saltwater intrusion map shows what weak systems do to long-term planning.

From maintenance event to maintenance window

Once I frame it that way, the value proposition becomes much richer. We are not only selling a stronger install. We are selling earlier knowledge, more graceful maintenance, and the possibility of preserving service continuity even when work has to happen. That is a very different standard than the industry has been used to buying.

Why better transition materials matter

That distinction matters anywhere purity is part of the value proposition: flood zones where contaminated water can press against a drinking-water main, coastal corridors where salinity keeps attacking every weakness, sewer-adjacent trenches where pressure transients can invite intrusion during low-pressure events, subsea installations where external pressure and movement are relentless, and future life-support loops where contamination is not a nuisance but a survival risk.

Chapter 9 - The Cost of Certainty

"Savings in infrastructure are tomorrow's resilience budget." — Abel Jiménez

Figure 9.1. Earlier field verification turns doubt into a manageable engineering cost instead of a later public disruption.

Executives often experience testing as a technical checkbox. I see it as something more revealing. Testing shows what a system does and does not trust about itself, and it exposes how much the industry is paying for uncertainty.

The wider the gap between what the industry hopes is true and what it can actually prove, the more expensive certainty becomes. That is why localized confidence matters so much. If certainty can be bought closer to the point of risk, the burden on the broader system begins to shrink.

Testing as a mirror of distrust

I learned that the cost of certainty is often hidden in planning, permitting, and system operations through conversations tied to water and public infrastructure. EPA's Clean Water Act summary shows how compliance is structured around discharge control and operating discipline. MWRA and NEWIN show the scale and financial gravity of water systems that must keep functioning while projects are planned, funded, and executed. When systems cannot trust their interfaces efficiently, they do not just spend more on testing; they spend more on coordination, downtime, documentation, and delay.

This is why the economics of testing deserve more attention in public infrastructure debates. Politicians and boards often focus on replacement cost and headline capital cost while ignoring the recurring burden of proving, restoring, and defending system integrity. But those burdens affect schedules, budgets, labor planning, and the appetite for modernization. A system that buys certainty expensively becomes conservative for understandable reasons. It cannot afford many surprises.

Figure 9.2. Broad testing becomes expensive when a whole exposed system must prove what a smaller, local uncertainty actually controls.

Operational parallels from smart buildings

Practical transition work offers the useful analogy again. Good systems reduce expensive guesswork when operators get better information at the right points and when solutions fit real-world constraints instead of idealized assumptions.

Why this changes adoption dynamics

Lowering the cost of certainty matters because it speeds other decisions. Operators are more willing to modernize when they can trust the installation path. Contractors are more willing to build capability when the standard is clear. Regulators are more comfortable when the basis for confidence is stronger and better documented. In other words, certainty is not only a cost variable. It is an adoption variable. If this chapter has a larger strategic point, it is that knowledge architecture is part of infrastructure design. A system that learns more intelligently becomes cheaper to govern and easier to improve.

Pressure testing is expensive because it is buying confidence the hard way

Conventional pipeline testing concentrates cost because it asks the whole system to prove what often comes down to a much smaller uncertainty. The original plan behind SolidMelt captured this with unusual candor. It described the current practice of hydrostatic testing whole water lines, leaving long trench sections exposed, visually hunting leaks, pumping water out, repairing, and starting again. It also cited an example from PG&E where pressure testing in 2011 reportedly ranged from $125,000 to $500,000 per mile. Even if we treat that as a specific historical example rather than a universal rule, the underlying message stands: broad testing is expensive because it mobilizes broad risk.

Pneumatic testing can be even more politically sensitive because the stored energy in compressed gas raises the consequence of a failure. That is one reason the Bayonne accident is worth remembering. Workers there were injured while testing pipes with air. The issue is not that pneumatic testing is never allowed or never useful. The issue is that the more energy and volume we involve in a test, the more the test itself becomes part of the hazard landscape.

When cold weather monetizes neglect

Winter is one of the clearest ways infrastructure explains itself. In mild weather, a city can live with hidden weakness longer than it should. In extreme cold, the hidden weakness sends an invoice immediately. That is why I keep coming back to water-main failures in winter. They are not just utility events. They are concentrated lessons in how deferred maintenance, brittle materials, traffic control, emergency labor, and lost service all stack together at once.

WSSC Water's public winter-readiness materials make this visible in unusually direct terms. The utility says the chance of water-main breaks jumps by about 60 percent in cold weather compared with warmer months. It also reports that its crews repair nearly 1,800 water-main breaks and leaks on average each year. For fiscal year 2025, WSSC reported 2,259 water-main breaks and leaks, with repair costs of about $33 million. Of that, the winter period from November 2024 through February 2025 accounted for 1,496 breaks and roughly $22 million in repair cost. Those numbers matter because they show how quickly hidden weakness becomes public expenditure when temperature shock, older pipe, and service demand collide.

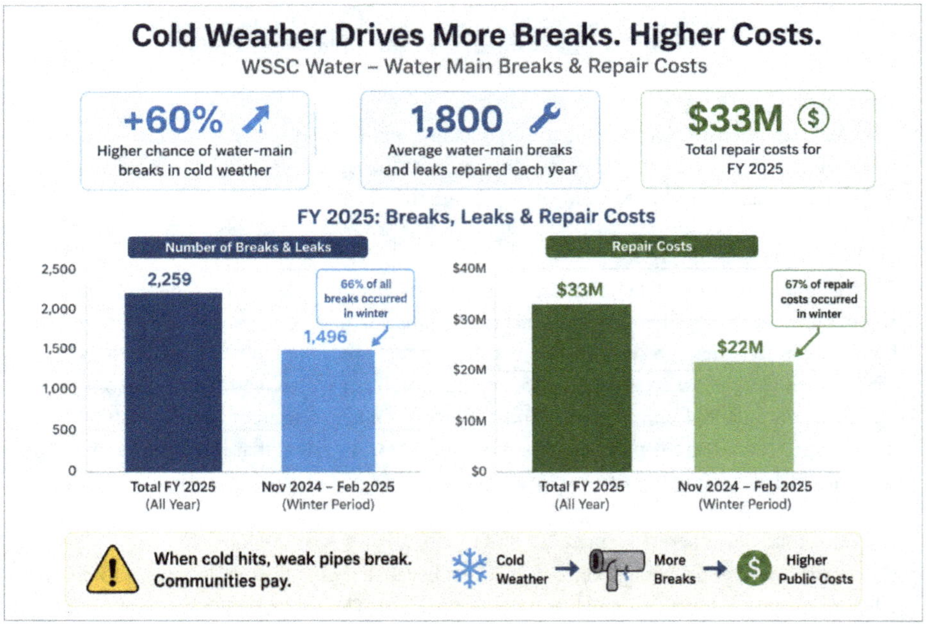

I have always thought those repair numbers understate the real cost. A broken main is not only a pipe problem. It is a traffic problem, a business interruption problem, a police-detail problem, a pavement restoration problem, a customer-communication problem, and often a liability problem. Streets stay open longer than anyone wants. Asphalt replacement and surface restoration get layered onto the invoice. Nearby contractors lose productivity waiting for the trench to clear. Residents lose water or deal with boil-water advisories, discoloration, or pressure drops. Even when the direct repair is handled quickly, the surrounding public cost can linger for days or weeks.

That is why I find the plan's language about progressive ditch closure, reduced detail officers, and reduced testing time so important. Those are not cosmetic advantages. They are cost drivers. If a crew can localize confidence and close a trench sooner, the public realm starts recovering sooner. If fewer sections need to stay open waiting for broad hydrotests or troubleshooting, then the total cost of install begins to move in the right direction before we even talk about the long-term maintenance savings. The SolidMelt development plan makes this case directly when it says immediate benefits in bidding come from reduced pressure-testing time, the ability to progressively close ditches, and lower need for costly details while excavations remain open.

Beyond the repair invoice

That is why I think earlier warning and more intelligible interfaces matter so much. Every minute saved in diagnosis, every segment isolated faster, and every trench closed earlier prevents secondary cost from mushrooming. This is also why I keep returning to the difference between direct repair cost and social cost. The city and the utility may carry one budget line, but residents, businesses, commuters, and emergency services carry others. A lower-loss, more maintainable standard is one of the few ways to reduce those invisible invoices before they ever show up.

Call to action: Calculate the full cost of uncertainty for one section of infrastructure—including testing, delay, rework, excavation, and service risk. Once we price doubt honestly, better options become easier to defend.

Chapter 10 - Why the Industry Will Resist Saving Money

"No new energy dependencies emerge." — Emmanuel Macron

Figure 10.1. Procurement teaches the market what to optimize for; better specifications reward outcomes instead of recurring invoices.

In every transformation I have worked on, resistance usually sounds more reasonable than it really is. Mature industries rarely say, 'we prefer inefficiency.' They say, 'we need more proof,' 'we need more time,' or 'this is not how we do it here.'

Markets say they reward efficiency, but mature industries often reward familiarity first. They reward established labor models, existing invoices, known procedures, and the quiet comfort of doing things the way everyone already understands. A new technology is welcomed when it adds value without disturbing the old structure. It becomes threatening when it removes friction that someone has learned to bill for.

The resistance will rarely present itself honestly. It will arrive as caution, due diligence, procurement inertia, concern about training, or appeals to existing standards. Some of those concerns will be legitimate. But mixed into them will often be something more ordinary: the instinct to protect the economics people already know how to survive inside.

The anatomy of resistance

Resistance becomes easier to understand when it is mapped by incentive rather than by stated rhetoric. The contractor worries about labor compression. The distributor worries about category disruption. The incumbent manufacturer worries about margin erosion. The inspector worries about new exposure. The utility worries about procurement risk. The regulator worries about headlines. The worker worries about skill displacement. Each concern may be presented as prudence, and some of it is prudence, but the pattern is not random. The system is defending the shapes of payment, authority, and familiarity it already knows how to manage.

Why coalition design matters

During my startup years, work connected to David Gardiner and Associates, NECEC, and CEBA reinforced a lesson that innovators often learn too late: opposition is rarely defeated by evidence alone. David Gardiner and Associates argues that community benefits agreements work best when they are transparent, public, and tied to tangible gains for host communities. NECEC's experience shows that even a large infrastructure project can become a referendum on trust, siting, and local benefit. CEBA shows that organized buyers can pull projects forward only when markets, rules, and counterparties are aligned.

This is not manipulation. It is transition design. People rarely oppose the future forever if they can see a respected place for themselves inside it.

What not to do

The worst rhetorical mistake an innovator can make is to present the industry as foolish for not changing sooner. That may feel emotionally satisfying, but it usually hardens opposition. Infrastructure people pride themselves on seriousness, memory, and risk awareness. If they feel mocked, they will become slower, not faster. A better strategy is to separate unnecessary waste from the dignity of the people who have had to work inside wasteful systems. Respect the field, but question the inherited cost structure. Respect the workers, but improve the workflow. Respect the need for proof, but redefine what proof can look like. This chapter's real argument is that reform succeeds not when it wins the abstract debate, but when it reorganizes survival in the new system.

Low bids, high maintenance, and the business of living with gaps

One of the most revealing things I heard in the field was how openly some people described the economics of inefficiency once they trusted the room. They told us that winning the first contract often means suppressing implementation cost aggressively, because everybody knows the project will later create opportunities in maintenance, repair, change orders, troubleshooting, restoration, and follow-on work. That is not a universal confession and I do not want to caricature the whole industry. But it is real enough that it changed how I think about resistance. The resistance to savings is not only ideological. It is embedded in the sequencing of revenue.

I think this is where founders make a critical mistake if they talk only about efficiency. Efficiency sounds like subtraction to people whose payroll depends on the current workflow. We have to talk instead about reallocating value. The market can still make money. Contractors can still win. Service providers can still grow. But more of the value will live in certified installation, monitoring, planned maintenance, data visibility, and long-term performance contracts, and less of it will live in emergency rework and prolonged uncertainty. If we do not say that clearly, people hear only the part of the future that seems to take something from them.

The low-bid business model in plain English

One of the most revealing things I heard during my startup years did not come from a polished conference stage. It came from real conversations with municipal leaders, field workers, utilities, contractors, and testing people who live inside these systems every day. Some of them said, quite openly, that large parts of the business still depend on the gaps and inefficiencies. The job gets priced to win the contract on the front end, and the maintenance, repair, change orders, or failure response help make up the margin later. It is not always said that bluntly in public, but once I heard it enough times, I could not unhear it.

That insight changed how I think about resistance. The problem is not just that procurement undervalues innovation. The problem is that some existing revenue models are built around the afterlife of imperfect installation and hard-to-verify systems. If a technology reduces uncertainty early, then it can take money away from the downstream friction that used to be monetized later. From the public side, that is a good thing. From the narrow perspective of a bidder trying to survive quarter to quarter, it can feel threatening.

The SolidMelt development plan captures this tension unusually well. It notes that common bidding practices often leave lifetime benefits and cost of ownership with little leverage and that the immediate selling points become reduced pressure-testing time, progressive ditch closure, and related short-term savings. But it also makes the more important strategic point: the real pricing goal should be based on total cost of ownership rather than lowest first cost. That is exactly the shift I believe public procurement still struggles to make.

We see the consequences everywhere. Cities end up with assets that looked cheap on award day and expensive every year after. Utilities are pushed to show near-term rate discipline even when a more durable system would lower lifetime cost. Contractors who know how to work inside the old friction have an advantage over contractors who would benefit from a cleaner standard but cannot yet count on owners to reward it. Then everyone says innovation is too expensive, when what they really mean is that innovation threatens a billing logic they already understand.

This is why I think we have to talk about contract structure and spec language, not just technical merit. If the specification only rewards immediate component price, then it teaches the market to ignore trench duration, testing burden, restoration time, service continuity, and maintenance frequency. If the specification instead rewards total cost of install, speed of restoration, ability to localize testing, reduced exposure to open ditches, lower future maintenance burden, and better long-term integrity, then the market begins pricing the right things. The same field that once treated inefficiency as inevitable starts treating it as expensive.

I do not say this to vilify contractors or utilities. Most people inside the system are reacting rationally to the signals they are given. If the owner pays for first cost and later treats maintenance as a separate problem, then the market will optimize around that split. If the owner starts buying performance over life of asset, then the market will adapt to that too. Resistance is often less about bad actors than about badly aligned incentives that have been normalized for decades.

For me, this is one of the most important fights in the whole book. If we do not fix the low-bid trap, we will keep rebuilding expensive weakness and congratulating ourselves for saving money on bid day. That is not thrift. It is deferred cost wearing the mask of discipline.

Procurement must learn to buy outcomes

I think public owners and regulated utilities will have to become more explicit about this if they want the market to change. If the bid is written for lowest purchase price, the market will give us lowest purchase price. If the bid is written for shortest restoration window, lower maintenance burden, lower test exposure, and lower lifetime disruption, the market will start giving us that instead. Procurement is not neutral. It teaches the market what to optimize for.

That is why I do not see specification language as boring back-office detail. I see it as one of the main battlegrounds of reform. A better future is often only one rewritten RFP away from becoming easier to finance, easier to justify, and easier to repeat.

Call to action: Rewrite one procurement or specification conversation so it rewards total cost of ownership instead of the cheapest first number. A better future usually begins when we buy outcomes instead of invoices.

Chapter 11 - Jobs, Standards, and the New Labor Model

"The government is committed to creating green jobs." — William Ruto

Figure 11.1. Training and certification turn new materials from a technical promise into trusted field practice.

I do not believe the future of infrastructure is less human. I believe it has to be more disciplined, better trained, and more respectful of the people who will carry a new standard into the field.

MassCEC's workforce data makes this chapter tangible. The clean-energy economy grows when training, apprenticeships, and contractor pipelines grow with it. That lesson lines up with what I heard from Boston Building Trades and field crews across Massachusetts: workers do not fear higher standards; they fear transitions that ignore how new standards must be learned, staffed, and paid for.

The easiest lie told during industrial change is that better systems destroy work. In reality, they usually destroy wasteful work first: rework, callbacks, emergency excavation, broad defensive testing, and the human effort required to compensate for systems that are not sufficiently trusted.

From failure labor to integrity labor

The new labor model matters because industries become humane or cruel partly through what they ask workers to spend their lives doing. A failure-driven labor model makes too much of its money from urgency, interruption, and costly disorder. Workers become experts at responding to crises that a better system should have made less common. An integrity-driven labor model shifts value toward training, certification, monitoring, documented installation, predictive maintenance, and continuous improvement. That does not erase labor. It dignifies it differently.

Sector examples

Housing and building sectors again provide relevant parallels. WinnCompanies' portfolio-scale sustainability work, Open Market ESCO's focus on advancing energy project financing and clean-energy solutions, and data-rich operating ecosystems all point toward a future in which recurring service, performance data, and long-term operating competence matter more than one-time heroic fixes. That same evolution can occur in water, gas, and pipeline work. More value can move into high-skill installation, leak detection, analytics, lifecycle service agreements, and documented quality assurance.

The political importance of this point is hard to overstate. People are much more willing to support system change when the new system appears to create better work rather than just eliminate familiar work. The labor story is therefore not a side issue. It is part of how the standard becomes socially acceptable.

Workforce as adoption infrastructure

What matters to me is that workforce development functions as adoption infrastructure. A technology can be brilliant and still fail if the workforce around it cannot install it, maintain it, explain it, and build trust in it.

Integrity work is higher-value work

When I imagine the labor market that would grow around SolidMelt, I do not imagine fewer skilled people. I imagine a different distribution of skill. I imagine more certified installers, more testing specialists, more monitoring technicians, more asset-management analysts, more maintenance planners, more marine and coastal installation experts, and more inspectors whose work has clear digital and operational consequences. In other words, I imagine moving labor away from low-trust emergency response and toward high-trust infrastructure stewardship.

Training, unions, and field discipline are part of the innovation

The more time I spent around utilities, testing organizations, manufacturers, labor groups, and municipal field crews, the more I came to a conclusion that sounds almost obvious in retrospect: training is part of the product. A technology that depends on field integrity does not arrive fully formed when the box is opened. It arrives when the crew knows how to prepare the pipe, align the work, execute the fusion correctly, document the outcome, and recognize what a pass, a warning, or a repair condition really means.

That is why I have never been persuaded by the lazy version of innovation rhetoric that says a better device will simply "disrupt" the field. Serious infrastructure does not work that way. It succeeds when the people who install, inspect, and maintain the system can take pride in a higher standard and can see a future for their own skills inside it. What I heard from Boston Building Trades, from utility personnel, and from experienced contractors was not fear of learning. It was fear of transitions that pretend learning is optional.

That is why I continue to see value in third-party testing culture, in authorization programs, in manufacturer training, in utility sign-off, and in the kind of field seriousness that many outsiders mistake for resistance. Often what looks like resistance is actually the field asking a fair question: who is going to stand behind this when the trench is closed and the public starts relying on it? The right answer is not "trust us." The right answer is a whole ecosystem of preparation, qualification, documentation, and ongoing support.

A higher standard needs visible pathways

One practical lesson I keep taking from workforce conversations is that people support higher standards faster when the pathway is visible. Show me the credential. Show me the training hours. Show me the authorization process. Show me how the contractor wins more work. Show me how the utility gets better documentation. Show me how the worker earns more trust and not just more responsibility. When those pieces are clear, adoption stops feeling like vague disruption and starts feeling like career structure.

That is another reason I believe training and certification belong inside the business model, not beside it. They are what turns a technical promise into a field reality people can organize around.

Call to action: Support one training, certification, or workforce pathway that turns lower-value repair work into higher-trust installation, monitoring, or maintenance work. The strongest standards create better jobs, not weaker ones.

Chapter 12 - Lowering the Cost of Everything

"We need predictable prices and structurally lower prices." — *Ursula von der Leyen*

This chapter is written for anyone trying to connect infrastructure to affordability in a serious way. Lowering the cost of life is not about slogans. It is about removing the hidden taxes that weak systems impose every day.

Every age believes its inflation is complicated, and in one sense it is. But beneath many pricing pressures sits a simpler truth: the world becomes expensive when too much value is lost between creation and use.

The official cost floor is already above one trillion dollars

When I convert the federal infrastructure surveys into one baseline, the first thing I see is that the country is already in a trillion-dollar catch-up cycle. The Environmental Protection Agency's Seventh Drinking Water Infrastructure Needs Survey puts drinking-water need at \$625 billion over twenty years. The 2022 Clean Watersheds Needs Survey adds another \$630.1 billion for wastewater, stormwater, and related clean-water need over the same period. That is a combined official floor of \$1.255 trillion, or about \$62.8 billion per year before inflation.

Figure 12.1. Street-level repair work shows how hidden infrastructure taxes reach city budgets, businesses, and residents.

Research support: water affordability is already a national finance problem

- Clean Water Action argues that safe, affordable drinking water is tied to public health, environmental justice, and economic stability, while aging infrastructure, source-water pollution, and rising utility costs threaten access.
- The same paper says SRF programs have dedicated more than $200 billion in financing support and that U.S. water infrastructure need exceeds $1 trillion over the next two decades.
- Implication for this book: total cost of ownership belongs in procurement because every avoidable failure competes with already-scarce public capital.

Source: Clean Water Action, Putting Drinking Water First.

What the city budgets are already telling us

The local examples tell the same story in more painful detail. In New York City, the Water Board's FY2026 adopted budget requires $4.615 billion in utility revenue. About 51.2 percent of that recoverable revenue goes to city operations, maintenance, and lease-related payments, while another 47.3 percent goes to financing and capital-related payments through the water finance structure. The combined metered water-and-sewer rate rose from $9.27 per 100 cubic feet in FY2014 to $13.07 in FY2026, a 41.0 percent increase. Once a system is carrying that much fixed cost, the argument for lower-loss installation becomes much stronger because every avoidable repair is now colliding with a rate base that is already under pressure.

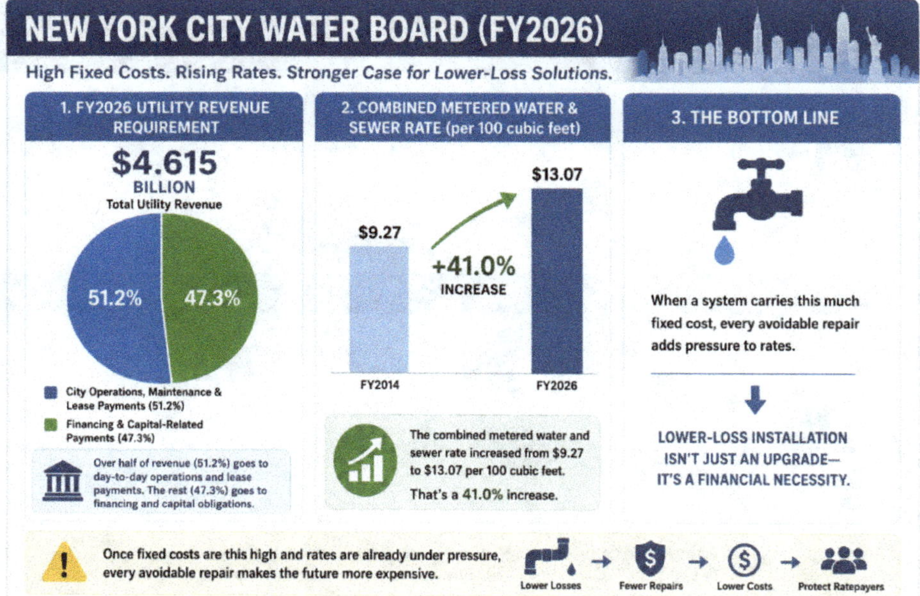

Greater Boston shows a different version of the same burden. The Massachusetts Water Resources Authority says its wholesale charges typically make up about 45 percent of what member communities bill their customers. Boston Water and Sewer Commission's 2025 proposed rate document says the MWRA assessment alone was budgeted at $264.3 million, or about 54.8 percent of total expenses. In the Authority's FY2026 final budget materials, projected rate revenue rises from $855.5 million in FY2025 to $988.9 million by FY2030, while the sample household bill used in the projections rises from $1,424 to $1,754, an increase of about 23.2 percent. That is not the profile of a system with room for repeated avoidable rework.

WSSC Water gives me one of the clearest windows into how emergency repair starts eating the future. Its FY2026 approved budget is $1.8 billion and is supported by a 9.5 percent revenue enhancement. Yet in FY2025 alone the utility says it spent $33 million responding to 2,259 breaks and leaks, with $22 million of that in the four busiest winter months. That means two-thirds of the annual break-and-leak repair cost hit in a narrow winter window, and the three-year break-repair cost rose from $17 million in FY2023 to $33 million in FY2025. The utility's own cost-of-service study also shows debt service in the range of roughly one-third of total expenditures. A system with that profile does not need more hidden failure. It needs fewer late surprises.

Miami-Dade and Miami Beach show what happens when aging systems, wastewater mandates, and climate exposure begin to stack on top of one another. Miami-Dade's Water and Sewer Department says its multi-year capital improvement program totals $8.79 billion and includes a $1.6 billion federally mandated consent decree over fifteen years.

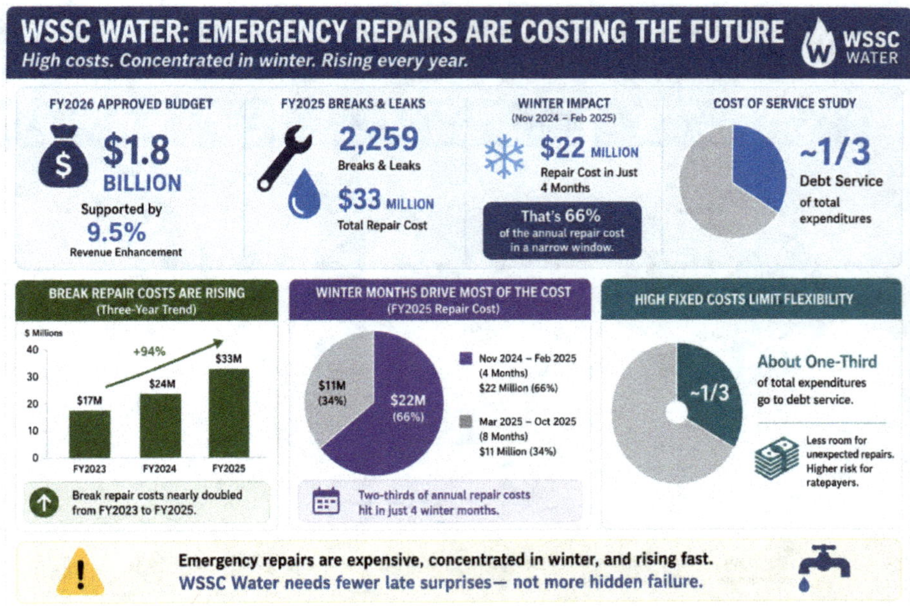

Miami Beach's FY2025/2026 utility notice shows the wholesale sewer pass-through rising 19.05 percent and the wholesale water pass-through rising 2.81 percent, pushing a sample combined residential bill from $97.73 to $105.65, an 8.1 percent increase in a single year. Once capital, compliance, and saltwater-intrusion risk begin to accumulate together, the value of non-porous, fused, lower-loss systems becomes easier to defend in purely financial terms.

Philadelphia's case is blunt and highly legible. The Philadelphia Water Department requested annual revenue increases of $73.63 million in FY2026 and another $69.34 million in FY2027. The official filing shows a typical monthly residential bill moving to $91.31 after the first increase and then to $96.68 after the second. Based on the department's own before-and-after bill figures, that is a cumulative increase of roughly 18.2 percent over the two-step period. Los Angeles shows the same pressure in different form. The Los Angeles Department of Water and Power's FY2025-2026 water budget totals $3.23 billion, with $1.153 billion in capital spending, about 35.7 percent of the budget, and $774 million in operations and maintenance, about 24.0 percent. The balance sits in financing, support, and other required functions. Again, this is the profile of a utility that must care about total cost of ownership, not merely first cost.

The point where basic service starts to break

This is the threshold I care about most. The Department of Energy classifies an energy burden of 6 percent or more of household income as high. The Environmental Protection Agency uses a 3 percent to 4.5 percent range to evaluate water affordability. Put together, those official thresholds imply that a household can cross into essential-service stress when home energy and water absorb roughly one-tenth of gross income. EPA now estimates that between 12.1 million and 19.2 million households already lack affordable access to water service. The first federal water-bill assistance program, the Low Income Household Water Assistance Program, ultimately served more than 1 million households and 1.5 million households by some program tallies, which tells me the affordability problem is not theoretical either.

This is why low-loss infrastructure deserves a more central place in cost-of-living conversations. It is one of the ways society converts technical discipline into public breathing room.

Illustrations from organizations and programs

In my startup years, different organizations illuminated different parts of the same argument. NECEC showed how affordability and clean infrastructure become politically meaningful when they are tied to reliability and consumer value. CEBA showed how buyer demand finances system change. MWRA and NEWIN showed that safe, affordable water depends on both physical integrity and capital readiness. HEET showed how invisible waste can be mapped and made impossible to ignore. CABA showed why pragmatic decarbonization matters in sectors that cannot wait for perfect future substitutes. David Gardiner and Associates showed that trust has to be designed into projects from the beginning.

Federal and nonprofit programs aimed at building efficiency and heat resilience often justify themselves in exactly these terms: lower utility costs, stronger resilience, and more room for communities to redirect scarce dollars to mission-focused work. The U.S. Department of Energy's (DOE) programs for efficient buildings and nonprofits, heat resilience initiatives, and housing-sector sustainability efforts all reflect a growing consensus that the cheapest new resource is often the waste you prevent.

Re-greening, water security, and the economics of restoration

The Amazon reminds us that the cost of everything is inseparable from the condition of the living systems beneath the economy. EPA guidance on trees and vegetation emphasizes that plants cool the air, reduce heat-island effects, support water management, and improve air quality. The same basic logic scales from city blocks to watersheds and from watersheds to continents: vegetation is not decoration. It is operating infrastructure for a livable climate.

That is why restoration and re-planting belong inside this argument. The world cannot keep stripping away forests, vegetation, and watershed resilience while pretending the bill will never arrive. Fewer trees mean hotter surfaces, weaker local moisture cycles, greater runoff, higher water stress, worse air quality, and more expensive adaptation. Re-vegetation is therefore not sentimental environmentalism. It is long-term systems maintenance for the only atmosphere humanity has.

Snow drought is now a pipe story too

The latest western snow data forces me to make this chapter much more concrete than I originally imagined. NOAA's National Integrated Drought Information System (NIDIS) partners reported in March 2026 that every major river basin in the West was in snow drought. Climate Central's April 1 analysis said western snow water equivalent was 65 percent below the 1991-2020 normal, the lowest on record for that time of year. NASA described the same season as a snow drought driven by warmth more than lack of precipitation. California's Department of Water Resources then reported on April 1 that statewide snowpack stood at only 18 percent of average and that there was no measurable snow at the critical Phillips

Station manual survey. These are not abstract climate statistics. They are early warnings about how much less natural water storage we can count on in the systems that feed cities and farms.

The Colorado River basin shows how large the stakes are. Reclamation repeatedly reminds us that the basin serves more than 40 million people, supports 5.5 million acres of agriculture, and underpins hydropower, tribal water supply, and environmental management across the West. California's Delta materials make a parallel point at a state scale: the State Water Project and Delta conveyance system help move water to roughly 27 million people and about 750,000 acres of farmland, and the state expects to lose around 10 percent of its water supply by 2040 under hotter and drier conditions. DWR says the future is likely to bring more rain, less snow, and more extreme swings, which means capturing water during infrequent big storms becomes more important, not less.

Once I put those pieces together, I see a future with more conveyance, not less. More regional interties. More tunnels, aqueduct upgrades, large-diameter replacement, sewer conversions, reuse pipelines, desalination discharge lines, agricultural distribution improvements, and emergency cross-connections. Some of that infrastructure will be controversial. Some of it will be delayed by politics. But the physics is moving ahead regardless. If less water is arriving in the form and place we historically expected, then more effort will go into moving, storing, segmenting, and protecting what we do get.

That is where SolidMelt becomes more than a utility niche. If the coming decades require us to build or rebuild a great deal of water infrastructure to sustain food systems and metropolitan demand, then the cost structure of pipe installation matters at a macro scale. We cannot afford to build twenty-first-century water conveyance with twentieth-century leak logic. We cannot keep financing kilometer after kilometer of new infrastructure only to leave the weakest interfaces as the least transparent parts of the system. And we certainly cannot treat testing, disruption, and maintenance as afterthoughts if the buildout ahead will be large.

Why water conveyance politics still point back to materials and infrastructure discipline

California's Delta Conveyance debate demonstrates the political edge of this issue. The project is controversial, expensive, and intensely scrutinized, yet DWR argues it is essential because the state faces less snow, more rain, and greater water instability. Whether one supports the exact project or not, the underlying lesson is hard to escape: climate adaptation is becoming a conveyance argument as much as a conservation argument. And whenever adaptation becomes a conveyance argument, pipe, tunnel, connection, and maintenance economics move to center stage. The smaller the hidden waste in those systems, the easier it is to defend the bigger public investment around them.

The water future of the American West is increasingly shaped by a contradiction that used to be easier to ignore. We still receive water, but we receive it in the wrong form, at the wrong time, and with less of the natural storage the old system depended on. Snowpack functioned as a slow-release reservoir. When that storage shrinks, melts early, or never forms, the entire downstream economy starts to strain: cities, hydropower, ecosystems, and agriculture all compete for a moving target instead of a predictable seasonal bank account.

The latest snow-drought reporting makes this more than a theoretical climate trend. In 2026, NOAA's drought center reported snow drought across every western state and every major western basin. California's Department of Water Resources described April 1 snowpack at a tiny fraction of average and noted that no measurable snow remained at its flagship Sierra survey site at a time of year when the state historically depends on snowmelt to carry water into the warm season. NASA has been documenting the same broad reality: the West is increasingly dealing with warm winters that erase natural storage before communities can rely on it.

Agriculture is central to this story. In the Colorado basin, agriculture uses the majority of developed water. In California, irrigation and food processing economies rely on a highly engineered storage-and-delivery network that was designed for a climate that is already shifting. When reservoirs run low, farmers do not simply plant less and call it a day. Entire regional economies feel the effects: cropping choices, groundwater pumping, food prices, labor demand, ecosystem tradeoffs, and urban-rural political conflict. A world with less dependable snowpack is a world that will be forced to move water more intentionally.

That means more pipelines, more canals, more interties, more recycled-water corridors, more groundwater-recharge conveyance, and more segmented infrastructure that can respond quickly when systems need repair. I do not say every solution is a giant pipeline. Some places need watershed restoration, demand management, and reuse before they need new long-haul assets. But I do say that the era of assuming existing conveyance is enough has ended. The food system will not tolerate that assumption for long.

Remote water access is economic development in its purest form

The development case is bigger than a water-utility case. UNICEF's latest global data show that 2.1 billion people still lack safely managed drinking water. UNESCO reports that women are responsible for collecting water in more than 70 percent of unserved rural households and spend 250 million hours every day doing it. The Gates Foundation notes that more than 3.5 billion people still live without safely managed sanitation. When I line those facts up, I do not see a marginal niche. I see one of the largest suppressed productivity stories in the world.

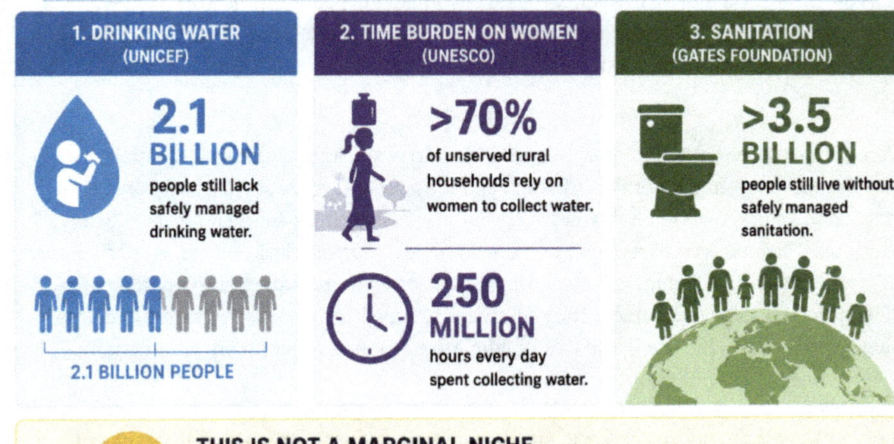

That is why I keep saying there is no meaningful limit to where lower-loss infrastructure can create value. The smart question is not whether remote development is possible. The smart question is where to start first so the savings are easiest to prove. I would begin where time poverty, weak hygiene, agricultural promise, and infrastructure underinvestment already overlap. Those are the places where every dollar of avoided failure does double work: it lowers engineering cost and unlocks human time.

What reliable water pressure buys first

A rural water line does not only deliver water. It delivers time, hygiene, school attendance, safer childbirth, cleaner utensils, better food preparation, and the basic dignity of washing every day without treating water as a scarce luxury. The World Health Organization says safe water, sanitation, and hygiene contribute not only to health but to livelihoods, school attendance, dignity, and resilient communities. That matters because the first visible return on infrastructure is often not industrial output. It is human energy that no longer has to be spent hauling survival home by hand.

Research support: inspection technology can turn hidden loss into visible work

- Solinas describes robotic pipeline inspection with HD cameras, laser profiling, gradient measurement, AI defect detection, and pipeline access across multiple diameter ranges.
- One Solinas showcase says inspection duration fell from 3 days to 1 day, with a five-fold reduction in cost and pits dug, and water access restored to 700 houses and 3,700 people.
- Implication for this book: lower-loss infrastructure is also an information problem - know sooner, dig less, and restore service faster.

Source: Solinas Endobot and Pipeline Inspection pages.

One of the clearest field studies I have seen came from rural Zambia. World Vision's evidence review found that households receiving piped water spent a median of 3.8 hours less per week fetching water, increased household water consumption by 32 percent, and used part of that gain for more gardening and productive household activity. That is what I mean by economic development in its most direct form. A line in the ground becomes time, health, and enterprise above ground.

The larger development institutions are already funding this logic at scale. In Karnataka, the World Bank approved financing aimed at bringing household piped drinking-water connections to around 2 million rural households—roughly 10 million people. In Ethiopia, the Bank describes rural piped systems designed to reach nearly 950,000 people through 110 systems. In Bangladesh, the Bank approved a program to help about 600,000 rural people gain safe water and more than 3.6 million gain improved sanitation. I read these not as isolated aid projects but as proof that the development world already understands the direction of travel.

Latin America has learned related lessons through information systems like SIASAR, which has been used across the region, including Costa Rica, to track rural water sustainability. That matters to me personally. Costa Rica taught me the moral case for stewardship, and SIASAR-style thinking reinforces the operational case: remote systems do not fail only because they are remote. They fail because too often they are installed without the visibility, maintenance planning, and cost discipline that make service durable.

The stack that turns a remote place into an economic oasis

Once water arrives reliably, other systems start making sense. The Food and Agriculture Organization's work on solar-powered irrigation shows that solar pumping can provide reliable and affordable energy for water access and agricultural production, especially where diesel is expensive and grid access is unreliable. The same work notes that these systems can also power mills, water purification, and cold storage. That is the beginning of a different rural economics: water for households, energy for pumps, refrigeration for food and medicines, and productive use that lifts incomes rather than merely holding survival together.

The Gates Foundation's sanitation work reinforces the same multiplier logic. The foundation says more than 3.5 billion people live without safely managed sanitation, that every dollar spent on sanitation can generate at least five dollars in economic return, and that it has already helped push more than 25 sanitation innovations toward licensing, production, and commercialization. That is exactly the kind of ecosystem logic I want readers to see. Water lines, toilets, washing stations, power, clinics, schools, and enterprise are not separate moral projects. They are one development architecture.

Vaccines, clinics, and the hygiene systems beneath health

I also want to make one connection that is often missed when people talk about global health. Vaccination campaigns, maternal care, and primary care do not float above infrastructure. They sit on it. In 2024, the World Health Organization, UNICEF, Gavi, and the Gates Foundation highlighted that immunization efforts have saved at least 154 million lives over the past fifty years. That achievement is enormous, but it still depends on clinics that can wash hands, clean surfaces, protect waste streams, and operate with safe water and dependable power.

WHO and UNICEF reported that half of health-care facilities globally still lack basic hygiene services, putting about 3.85 billion people at greater risk, while UNICEF says 2.3 billion people still lack a handwashing facility with soap and water at home. I do not need to stretch those facts to make the point. A low-loss pipeline and a protected water network do not replace nurses, vaccines, or public-health leadership. But they make those interventions safer, more scalable, and more humane in places where the basics still fail too often.

The remote-development argument therefore does not compete with the urban savings case in this book. It completes it. Large cities show where hidden waste already crushes budgets. Remote regions show where saving that waste can create whole new layers of health, agriculture, education, and enterprise that were previously priced out. There really is no meaningful ceiling on where development can go when safe water, usable pressure, and affordable integrity finally arrive together.

Food security is becoming a water-conveyance problem

If we want to understand where infrastructure demand is heading, we have to follow food. Agriculture depends on timing, volume, quality, and reliability of water. When snowpack disappears early, when reservoirs swing harder, when groundwater is overdrawn, or when rivers are managed more aggressively to store upstream, cities and farms do not simply "use less" and move on. They build interties. They expand reuse. They fight over allocations. They modernize canals. They add pumping, storage, and conveyance. In other words, they become more dependent on infrastructure.

California offers the clearest current example. The Department of Water Resources has said that snowpack is a huge component of California's water system and that, on average, the Sierra snowpack supplies about 30 percent of the water Californians use. But DWR has also been forced to talk more openly about a future with less snow, more rain, and earlier runoff.

That shift matters because snow is not just water in frozen form; it is a timing mechanism. It releases supply gradually into spring and summer when farms, cities, ecosystems, and hydropower systems need it. When that timing collapses, storage and conveyance have to work harder.

That is the deeper meaning of projects like Delta conveyance. DWR describes the State Water Project as infrastructure that helps move water to more than 27 million Californians and about 750,000 acres of farmland. It has also argued that if the Delta Conveyance Project were already operating during the 2025 water year, about 956,000 acre-feet of water could have been captured so far. We can argue about design, governance, ecology, and politics, but the strategic message is plain: in a world of flashier storms and weaker snowpack, capture-and-move capability becomes more valuable, not less.

The same logic shows up across the Colorado River Basin. The Bureau of Reclamation describes a system supporting more than 40 million people and 5.5 million acres of agriculture. Once numbers get that large, conveyance cannot be treated as a side issue. Every leakage loss, every preventable outage, every major repair, and every avoidable maintenance cycle is multiplied across food systems, municipal systems, and energy systems at once. This is one reason I believe the future of food security is quietly becoming a pipe story.

I do not mean that pipelines replace better farming, conservation, recycling, groundwater recharge, or landscape restoration. We need all of those. What I mean is that as drought variability intensifies and the hydrologic calendar becomes less stable, the physical movement of water becomes more strategic. Cities are already capturing stormwater, reusing wastewater, recycling more aggressively, building groundwater recharge projects, and looking for ways to hold onto high-quality water when it is available. Agriculture is already adapting through crop shifts, efficiency investments, district coordination, and political battles over timing and allocation. Each of those responses leans more heavily on infrastructure.

That is where I think SolidMelt belongs in the conversation. If the coming decades require more reuse lines, more agricultural interties, more district-to-district resilience, more coastal adaptation, more desalination support lines, and more long-haul or regional conveyance, then lowering the total cost of install and the total cost of ownership becomes a strategic question, not just a project-management question. The plan's emphasis on reduced testing time, progressive ditch closure, reduced disruption, and lifetime value is not just nice economics. It is exactly the kind of economics water-stressed regions will need if they are going to expand infrastructure without making every new line politically unaffordable.

I also think we need to say out loud what people often imply only indirectly: snow drought is here now. It is no longer a hypothetical. NOAA's drought and snowpack tracking, NASA's Earth-observing work, and state agencies in the West are all telling versions of the same story. Warm winters, thinner snowpacks, earlier melt, and more volatile runoff are already changing planning assumptions. That does not mean every reservoir will be empty every year. It means reliability itself becomes more expensive to produce, and that pushes societies toward more built conveyance, more reuse, and more interconnection.

Call to action: Map one hidden infrastructure tax that is flowing into rates, food costs, public works, or operating budgets. When we name the friction clearly, we can finally start removing it.

Chapter 13 - Why People Will Fight the Right Thing

"Innovation is the answer to unemployment." — *William Ruto*

One lesson I carried from startup work and large transformations alike is that good ideas are not fought only because they are wrong. They are also fought because they expose the economics and habits people have learned to depend on.

People do not fight only what is wrong. They also fight what is right when what is right threatens the structure of their current advantage. That is why reform is rarely opposed only by ignorance. It is opposed by position.

A better system can expose the old one too clearly. Once a lower-loss path becomes visible, legacy weaknesses stop looking like fate and start looking like choice. That is uncomfortable for organizations, professions, and industries that have spent years normalizing the costs of uncertainty.

The answer is not contempt for the people inside the old system. It is strategy. Reform survives when it offers those people a role in the new order and proves that lower waste does not destroy the future - it redistributes it.

Why right answers provoke resistance

People fight the right thing when the right thing exposes that the old burden was never as inevitable as they told themselves. That exposure is more than intellectual. It can feel moral, status-related, and economic all at once. A better standard does not merely promise improvement; it also casts retrospective light on all the unnecessary cost the old standard normalized. That is one reason reform can feel accusatory even when no accusation is spoken aloud. It changes what counts as excusable.

Heat and climate as an example of social learning

Heat resilience offers a wider civic analogy. Communities once treated extreme heat as a seasonal inconvenience rather than a complex public-health and infrastructure issue. Over time, research, monitoring, and community programs changed that understanding. Now heat is increasingly managed as a serious systems issue involving data, public communication, preparedness, and local adaptation. Social learning changed what counts as normal, acceptable, and urgent.

Strategy over mere evidence

I saw this dynamic repeatedly when working with startup-adjacent coalitions and public-interest organizations. HEET's leak maps are powerful not only because they provide evidence, but because they make that evidence visible in neighborhoods, around schools, and in places people care about. David Gardiner and Associates' writing on community benefits makes a parallel point: evidence changes behavior more effectively when communities can see what they gain, how agreements are enforced, and who is accountable.

This is why I insist that truth must arrive with strategy. It is not enough to demonstrate that lower loss is good. Reformers have to understand the emotional, organizational, and economic structures that make people cling to preventable weakness. They have to provide bridges, roles, and professional pathways into the new system. And they have to keep repeating that lower waste does not mean lower value for society; it means value is migrating out of recurring failure and into more productive forms. The right thing wins only when it becomes survivable for enough people to stop fighting it.

Water politics shows why even obvious projects get fought

Conveyance politics offer one of the clearest examples of why people fight the right thing. Projects can be obviously connected to resilience and still face years of delay because costs are front-loaded while benefits are distributed, because disruption is local while reliability is regional, and because trust in the implementing institutions is usually lower than trust in the status quo people already know how to criticize. I see the same pattern in utility replacement work, sewer conversions, and gas modernization. The public often agrees something is broken. What it does not yet trust is that the fix will be competent, fair, and worth the disruption.

Miami shows how denial becomes a budget line

If I wanted one city to explain why people fight the right thing, I could do worse than point to Miami. South Florida gives us a brutally practical lesson in what happens when geology, sea-level rise, water quality, wastewater, and public finance start colliding at the same time. The challenge is not a single dramatic event. It is a stacked systems problem: porous limestone, rising groundwater, saltwater intrusion into the Biscayne Aquifer, king-tide flooding, stormwater that cannot drain the way it used to, and septic systems that become less reliable as groundwater rises.

Miami-Dade's own public materials say the Biscayne Aquifer, the county's primary source of drinking water, is vulnerable to saltwater intrusion. The City of Miami's sea-level-rise materials describe how rising seas push groundwater upward through the porous limestone base and reduce the ability of stormwater systems to function the way they were designed.

County materials also note that contamination introduced through septic systems can migrate through groundwater toward canals, Biscayne Bay, and other water resources. In other words, the region is living through a case study in why clean-water systems, dirty-water systems, drainage systems, and coastal climate risk cannot be managed as separate silos anymore.

And yet even when the problem is obvious, the right response is still hard to build. Sewer conversions cost money. Stormwater upgrades cost money. Coastal adaptation projects cost money. Saltwater-intrusion barriers, pumping changes, backflow controls, and groundwater protection measures all cost money. Communities argue about who pays, where to prioritize, how fast to move, and whether current property owners should absorb the burden of future protection. This is exactly the kind of setting where people fight the right thing not because they cannot see the problem, but because the solution redistributes cost and responsibility.

That is also why I keep coming back to material choice. Coastal regions are punishing environments. Corrosion is relentless. Groundwater conditions are complicated. Salinity changes the maintenance equation. The case for HDPE in those environments is not ideological. It is operational. The material's corrosion resistance, flexibility, long service life, and fused-system logic become more valuable when the surrounding environment is already trying to punish every weak point in the network. If I am rebuilding in a coastal zone where groundwater and salinity are part of daily reality, I do not want a system that asks me to fight corrosion forever.

But even there, the old trap remains. If procurement looks only at first cost, then we can still make short-term decisions that guarantee long-term pain. If project logic ignores testing burden, disruption, maintenance, and service continuity, then we can still spend large sums rebuilding vulnerability into the coast. That is why I think Miami belongs in this chapter. It shows that even when the physical evidence is visible on streets, in drainage systems, and in aquifer management, the political system can still hesitate because the right answer is capital-intensive up front and disruptive to familiar arrangements.

That is why Miami is such a useful counterargument to complacency. It shows us that the right thing can be obvious physically and difficult politically at the same time. The work, then, is not merely to prove the engineering. It is to prove that the better system lowers the whole civic burden enough that resistance slowly loses its best excuse.

Integrity cannot replace consent, but it can narrow risk

Some infrastructure conflicts are not primarily engineering conflicts. They are sovereignty, trust, history, and land-use conflicts. The Dakota Access fight became a global example because the Standing Rock Sioux argued that the line threatened water and sacred sites near Lake Oahe and the Missouri River. Michigan's Line 5 battles show the same pattern in another form. After the Marshall spill, cleanup was estimated at more than one billion dollars, and the state later required additional underwater monitoring technologies, weather-related shutdown criteria, and other safeguards for the Straits section because people no longer accepted blind trust as a substitute for proof.

That is why I pay attention to community and Indigenous monitoring models. The Canada Energy Regulator says its Indigenous monitoring program is meant to strengthen safety and environmental oversight, prevent harm, help protect Indigenous interests, and build relationships. Its Indigenous Advisory and Monitoring Committees for Trans Mountain and Line 3 were created so Indigenous peoples could participate meaningfully in oversight activities along the corridor while those projects are built and operated. Participation does not automatically mean support. It means oversight no longer belongs only to the owner.

I would never call that a complete answer. But I would call it a better starting point than asking communities to trust a company first and evidence second. Better monitoring does not replace consent. It gives future negotiations a more credible, more transparent, and potentially more shared model of accountability.

Call to action: Have one honest conversation with a stakeholder who fears losing margin, relevance, or control. Real change accelerates when we address what people are protecting, not just what they are resisting.

Chapter 14 - The World That Wastes Less

"Forests and oceans work in harmony to sustain the water cycle and regulate the climate." — Luiz Inácio Lula da Silva

I want to close this book the same way I try to lead change: by returning to stewardship. Every system reveals its values in what it tolerates, and the real question is not only what we can build next, but what we are finally disciplined enough to stop wasting.

In the startup chapter of my life, the organizations I worked with kept bringing me back to one shared insight. Whether the conversation was about transmission, power procurement, affordable water, methane leakage, or pragmatic fuels, the common thread was not ideology. It was stewardship. The future gets built when systems waste less and when the public can see that lower waste creates real economic and human value.

That is also why I continue to connect this argument to landscape restoration, trees, and long-term human survivability. We only have one atmosphere, one hydrologic cycle, and one biosphere to work with. Large-scale revegetation and replanting are not substitutes for better infrastructure, but they are part of the same moral logic: protect what keeps life possible, reduce preventable loss, and design systems that future generations can still afford to inherit.

Every civilization eventually reveals what it truly worships in what it is willing to waste. For too long, the modern world acted as though leakage, corrosion, over-testing, emergency repair, and hidden infrastructure friction were merely technical details. That age is ending.

The future belongs to the world that wastes less - less water, less gas, less oil, less labor, less doubt, less emergency response, and less value lost between creation and use. Waste is no longer a side effect. It is a verdict on design, standards, leadership, and the willingness of institutions to keep paying for preventable weakness.

Civilization is governed at the margin. When the connection holds, daily life feels ordinary. When it fails, the cost arrives everywhere. The world that preserves value more intelligently than it consumes it will be the world that remains most affordable, resilient, and worthy of trust.

The blue frontier: subsea infrastructure, information, and habitat

There is another frontier I should name plainly: the ocean. Humanity has spent centuries crowding the land, fighting over shorelines, and treating the sea mainly as a route, a resource field, or a dumping ground. Yet much of the modern world already depends on underwater infrastructure. NOAA notes that submarine cables carry a majority of civilian, military, and government offshore communications traffic, while the International Telecommunication Union says submarine cable systems carry roughly 99 percent of global Internet traffic.

The next step is not automatically underwater cities, and it would be irresponsible to pretend that such habitats are around the corner. But it is entirely reasonable to say that subsea infrastructure, immersed tunnels, offshore utility corridors, and highly automated integrity monitoring will become more important over time. Europe's Fehmarnbelt project shows that long immersed underwater tunnels are no longer science fiction. They are major civil-engineering works executed with modular fabrication, heavy monitoring, and long-term design discipline.

A world that wastes less is a world that can still afford to build

I keep coming back to buildability because that is what the next decades will demand from us. We will need to protect forests, replant vegetation, convert septic systems, harden coasts, modernize gas networks, replace lead and brittle water mains, expand reuse, and in some places construct entirely new conveyance corridors. Every one of those ambitions competes for money, labor, public tolerance, and materials. A society that wastes heavily inside its basic infrastructure cannot do many of those things at once. A society that lowers hidden failure cost can.

The blue frontier will reward integrity, not improvisation

I do not talk about subsea infrastructure because I think underwater life is around the corner in some simplistic science-fiction sense. I talk about it because the ocean is already an infrastructure domain, and it is going to become more important. NOAA has long emphasized the importance of submarine cables, which carry the overwhelming majority of intercontinental digital traffic. Europe is building the Fehmarnbelt immersed tunnel. Offshore wind, offshore transmission, marine monitoring, desalination, coastal protection, hydrogen corridors, carbon-management systems, and subsea data routes are all pushing human systems farther into marine environments. The blue frontier is not fantasy. It is already under construction.

That has implications far beyond oil. Imagine recycled-water conveyance crossing coastal shelves to serve island or peninsula communities. Imagine desalination support lines, district cooling loops, or protected subsea utility spines serving dense coastal cities. Imagine marine industrial parks or tunnel-linked logistics systems that need pressurized transport lines to move water, energy carriers, or cooling fluids safely. All of those systems will be judged not only by what they can carry, but by how gracefully they can fail, how quickly they can warn, and how little public disruption they create when maintenance finally has to happen.

This is one reason I sometimes say the future belongs to technologies that buy us time rather than only technologies that promise speed. Faster installation is useful, yes. Lower total cost is useful, yes. But earlier warning and cleaner isolation in high-pressure or high-consequence environments may ultimately be even more valuable. A society that can schedule maintenance before a defect becomes a catastrophe is a society that has learned how to live with infrastructure more intelligently.

Aquarius shows what survival infrastructure looks like underwater

If I want a real-world picture of why integrity matters underwater, I do not have to imagine a fantasy city under the sea. Aquarius Reef Base already gives me a smaller, more honest example. Florida International University describes Aquarius as relying on a life-support buoy that provides all of the essential utilities and communications to the underwater habitat, while mission control watches life-support data, communications, and science feeds around the clock. Even a short-duration underwater habitat depends on uninterrupted, trustworthy flows.

NOAA's own environmental review reminds me that the ocean already carries civilization's critical corridors. It says submarine cables carry about 99 percent of international communications traffic. That means society already trusts subsea corridors with data, power, and strategic connectivity. The problem is that our integrity discipline has not always kept up with our dependence. The Government Accountability Office found that federal offshore regulators do not have a robust oversight process for about 8,600 miles of active Gulf of Mexico pipelines and that the methods relied on are not always reliable for detecting ruptures.

Space is the same integrity argument with less forgiveness

Once we leave Earth, the argument becomes harsher. NASA says reliable life-support systems are critical because space means isolation, continuous exposures, reuse of air and water, and limited rescue options. Orion's closed-loop life-support system is designed to maintain a positive-pressure, breathable atmosphere for up to 144 hours even in the event of a pressure-vessel leak or a contaminated cabin atmosphere. On the International Space Station, NASA has now demonstrated 98 percent water recovery because every gallon launched from Earth is too valuable to waste.

What interests me most is that NASA is already thinking in pipeline terms. Its Lunar South Pole Oxygen Pipeline concept imagines transporting high-purity oxygen from extraction sites to storage or habitat areas because moving that oxygen by rover may be the most expensive part of the system. NASA's cryogenic fluid-management work makes the same point for liquid hydrogen, liquid oxygen, and liquid methane: future missions need better ways to store, transfer, and measure precious fluids over long durations and under extreme conditions.

The farther humans go from Earth, the less forgiving the environment becomes. There are no convenient truck rolls. There is no easy reroute. There is often no near-term rescue. So the same discipline I argue for in city streets becomes even more valuable at planetary distance:

better proof, earlier warning, protected purity, and maintenance planned before loss becomes catastrophe.

Data, pressure, and the next built environment

The more I think about subsea and cross-continental systems, the more I see that the future will depend on the same two disciplines repeated in new environments: segment what matters, and know sooner. We already accept those rules for data networks. We build redundancy, route around failure, and monitor constantly because waiting for a dramatic outage is too expensive. Physical fluid networks are moving in that direction as well. Remote sensing, isolation logic, and continuous integrity awareness will increasingly be the norm in high-value systems, not an exotic add-on.

Call to action: Set one measurable target for wasting less—water, energy, methane, maintenance time, or public money—and publish it. A world that wastes less begins with a promise that can be counted.

Chapter 15 - Global Sustainability Networks and the Bridge Economy

"GAoS: Global Leaders. Collective Action. Measurable Sustainability Impact." — Global Ambassadors of Sustainability

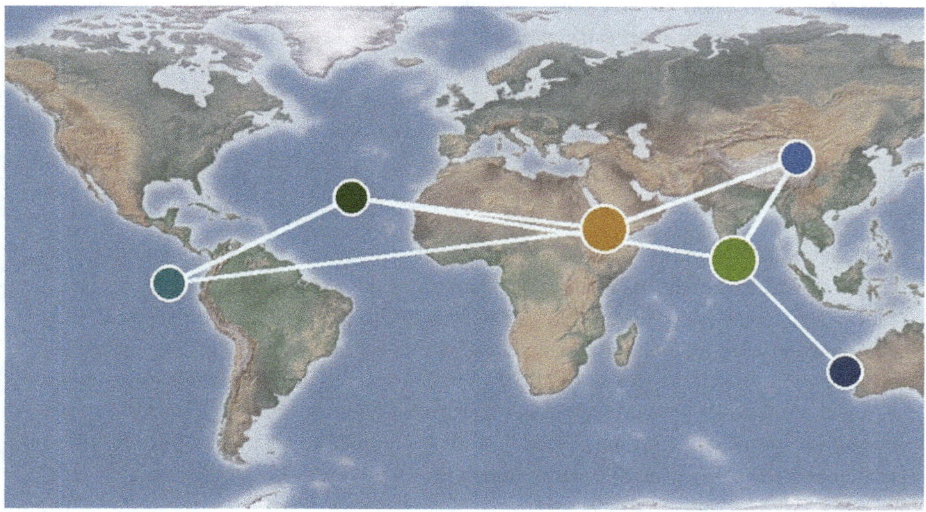

Figure 15.1. The bridge economy scales through networks that connect materials, training, procurement, finance, and measurable impact.

Research support: resource recovery turns wastewater into a value platform

- WEF describes its Resource Recovery Roadmaps as a high-level guide for utilities and decision-makers considering the NEW paradigm: nutrients, energy, and water.
- WEF's Resource Recovery Handbook covers water reuse, energy, nutrients, biosolids, utility decision-making, financial aspects, and long-term planning.
- Implication for this book: the bridge economy is not one product; it is the operating system that lets utilities recover more value from what used to be waste.

Sources: Water Environment Federation Resource Recovery Roadmaps and Resource Recovery Handbook.

The bridge to a greener economy will not be built by materials alone. It will be built by networks of people who can translate sustainability into procurement, manufacturing, education, investment, field execution, and daily life. That is why the Global Ambassadors of Sustainability belongs in this book. Its public materials describe GAoS as a nonprofit international network and think tank registered in Canada, with more than 13,000 members from 130 countries, focused on sustainability practices, climate action, and international partnerships. Its motto on LinkedIn is "Bringing People Together and Learn from Each Other."

The materials show recurring themes across the Global Ambassadors of Sustainability, the Global Green Chamber of Commerce, and partner sessions: green mindset, education-to-career pathways, water resilience, sponge cities, post-crisis recovery, nature-based systems, well-being economics, green reconstruction finance among others. GAoS reinforces one central point: the transition will not succeed as a sudden lifestyle disruption. It will succeed when better materials, better infrastructure, better education, better incentives, and better design make greener living the normal way life works.

The strongest theme from GAoS for this book is not a single slogan. It is the idea that green transformation must be practical, connected, and globally teachable. The GGSL Academy, a joint initiative of GAoS and the U.S. Green Chamber of Commerce, states a mission to provide accessible, globally recognized training and certification programs that build practical green competencies, foster leadership capacity, and support career pathways in the emerging green economy. That is exactly the kind of ecosystem required for the transition strategy I am arguing for here.

This matters for oil and carbon-based products because the real world does not move from legacy materials to green materials in one dramatic leap. It moves through bridges. The established carbon-based materials already embedded in pipe systems, medical products, packaging, insulation, transportation, renewable-energy supply chains, concrete additives, sensors, and industrial processes can be modified, improved, reused, recycled, and redeployed to lower waste while greener alternatives earn trust. If we reduce leakage, corrosion, rework, unnecessary transportation, and overbuilt repair cycles today, we buy time and capital for the next generation of greener materials tomorrow.

The International Committee of Social Entrepreneurship and Sustainability (ICSES), launched by GAoS and the Global Green Chamber of Commerce, frames social entrepreneurship as a way to combine business innovation with sustainability, inclusivity, and global equity. That language strengthens this book's argument that sustainability must become profitable, ordinary, and operational. A green future that requires people to abandon daily life will struggle. A green future that improves the materials, infrastructure, and purchasing decisions people already use can spread much faster.

That is the bridge economy: not a compromise with the past, but a disciplined way to use the present as the launchpad for the future. Petroleum-based and carbon-based products are not all the same. Some uses increase waste. Other uses can reduce much larger losses by making infrastructure more durable, cleaner, lighter, more corrosion-resistant, easier to maintain, or more efficient to transport. The practical question is not whether a molecule began in oil. The practical question is whether the product it becomes reduces net harm while the greener substitute is being developed and scaled.

This is where organizations like GAoS, CleanTech Open, Greentown Labs, MassCEC, CEBA, CABA, HEET, NEWIN, MWRA, David Gardiner and Associates, and others belong in one introduction. Each represents a different piece of the same puzzle: education, commercialization, clean-energy demand, pragmatic fuel pathways, methane visibility, water affordability, community trust, and policy alignment. The bridge strategy needs all of them because no single product, organization, government, or technology can carry the transition alone.

In practical terms, this chapter adds one more call to action. We should not wait until green materials are perfect before improving the carbon-based systems we already use. We should demand lower-loss carbon-based products now, more recyclable and more durable materials now, less leakage now, cleaner infrastructure now, and better standards now. Every improvement in the current system reduces the burden placed on the future system.

Call to action: Build the bridge. Improve the carbon-based products we already use, support the organizations training the next generation of sustainability leaders, and make greener living the default rather than a lifestyle exception.

Chapter 16 - Green Mindset, Water Resilience, and the Transition Culture

"Sustainability is not just technical. It is cognitive, spatial, and economic." — Global Ambassadors of Sustainability session framing

The green mindset is a design requirement

The Global Ambassadors of Sustainability add a useful missing layer to this book because they show how a transition actually becomes normal. The speakers do not treat sustainability as one product, one regulation, one building code, or one energy source. They describe it as a chain of habits, skills, incentives, materials, finance, infrastructure, and leadership decisions that must reinforce one another. That is also the argument of this book: oil- and petroleum-derived materials can help accelerate the transition when they are improved, redesigned, reused, measured, and governed as bridge tools rather than defended as excuses for waste.

This matters because the public is unlikely to accept a greener life if greener life feels like a punishment, a luxury, or a heroic exception. The transition becomes durable when better choices become easier, cheaper, more available, and more trusted than the old choices. Petroleum-based materials already sit inside the normal way of life. If we use that established base to manufacture longer-lived components, lower-loss infrastructure, cleaner water systems, more durable surfaces, better insulation, efficient transport systems, and recyclable products, then oil becomes part of the runway that helps greener technologies take off.

Anita Singa, principal at the Global Indian International School in Dubai, connected sustainability leadership to the formation of a green mindset. Her central point was that climate risk is systemic, leadership decisions are intergenerational, and a leader is remembered less for what was extracted than for what was protected. That lesson connects directly to this book. The transition from wasteful carbon use to disciplined carbon-based bridge materials will not happen because the chemistry alone is possible. It will happen when leaders decide that protection, efficiency, and long-term resilience belong inside procurement and product design from the beginning.

Figure 16.1. Transition culture begins with learning environments that make sustainability practical instead of performative.

Her Costa Rica example is especially important to me personally. She describes how Costa Rica moved from forest loss and biodiversity decline toward a policy-driven recovery that used ecosystem-service payments, legal protections, and sustainability incentives. The practical lesson is simple: what we reward determines what we protect. If we reward only low first cost, we will keep buying systems that waste money later. If we reward durability, lower emissions, repairability, reuse, and measurable performance, then oil-derived products can become tools of transition rather than tools of delay.

The built environment has to work for the nervous system

Dr. Marina Maria, founder of the Academy of Neuroscience for Cities, Environment and Design in Lebanon, pushed the conversation into neuroarchitecture. Her point was that sustainable buildings cannot be evaluated only by energy, water, and carbon metrics. They also have to support the body, the brain, stress regulation, attention, belonging, and well-being. If people feel uncomfortable in a building, they change the lighting, temperature, surfaces, and operating conditions until the original sustainability model fails in practice.

That insight matters for oil-based transition materials because materials are not only technical. They are experienced by people every day: in walls, floors, windows, pipes, coatings, insulation, furniture, packaging, vehicles, and public spaces. Carbon-based products can support the bridge to a greener life when they help buildings become healthier, quieter, better insulated, easier to maintain, and more compatible with the way people actually live. A material that saves energy but makes daily life uncomfortable will be resisted. A material that saves energy and improves comfort becomes part of a new normal.

Well-being economics exposes the hidden cost of waste

Emanuel Goodman Gates, founder and sustainability consultant at Capital Green Works in Denmark, framed the economic problem sharply. He explained that a conventional growth metric such as gross domestic product can miss what matters most: care work, ecosystem services, equity, distribution, and environmental damage. His Amazon example is directly relevant to this book. If a standing forest is treated as economically invisible while logging and cattle conversion count as output, the accounting system quietly rewards destruction. If oil-spill cleanup spending counts as economic activity without subtracting the ecological damage, the ledger is telling the wrong story.

The transition-materials argument depends on changing that accounting logic. We should not celebrate any carbon-based product merely because it creates sales. We should ask whether it reduces lifetime waste, preserves water, lowers energy demand, extends asset life, replaces a more harmful alternative, or makes green technologies easier to adopt. That is the bridge economy I want this book to defend: not growth for growth alone, but productive use that reduces the total damage and increases the total usefulness of the systems we already depend on.

Green careers are no longer a niche path

Miriam Larby, speaking from a governance and environmental, social, and governance perspective, described the green economy as the next phase of the global economy, not a niche sector. She identified three skills that matter for organizations trying to move from intent to action: the data architect, the system designer, and the ethical negotiator. That framework should sit near the center of this book. Improving today's oil- and carbon-based products requires all three.

The data architect measures emissions, life-cycle impacts, climate risk, energy use, water loss, and material performance. The system designer redesigns products, supply chains, infrastructure, and operating models so waste is reduced before it becomes a cost. The ethical negotiator brings boards, regulators, contractors, communities, investors, and workers into alignment. A transition built only by scientists will stall. A transition built only by activists will stall. A transition built by data, systems, and trust has a chance to become normal.

Universities and classrooms are part of the bridge

Dr. Connie Mitchell of Prince Sultan University emphasized that education cannot remain abstract if we want sustainable development to become real. Campuses can become living laboratories, curricula can embed the Sustainable Development Goals, and students can learn to solve traffic, air quality, water, and materials challenges as practical problems rather than distant ideals. Her closing idea was powerful: education is not only about preparing students for the world; it is about preparing students to save it.

That is why this book should not talk about carbon-based bridge materials as if they belong only to industry. They also belong to classrooms, trade schools, laboratories, municipal training programs, and business schools. If students learn how to improve existing materials while green alternatives scale, they can enter the workforce ready to reduce emissions immediately instead of waiting for perfect future materials. The transition becomes faster when the next generation learns to improve the systems already in front of them.

Water resilience proves that the bridge has to be physical

The water-resilience and sponge-city examples sharpen the physical side of this argument. Professor Uli from SRH University in Germany described a water-conscious city as one that captures, stores, infiltrates, reuses, and manages rainwater close to where it falls. Dr. Reham Fakuri described sustainable urban drainage strategies such as rainwater harvesting, permeable surfaces, filter strips, infiltration basins, green roofs, blue roofs, and constructed reed-bed systems. Those ideas show why the transition is not only about replacing fuels. It is about rebuilding the surfaces, storage, pipes, membranes, tanks, roofs, and urban systems that determine whether water becomes a hazard or a resource.

Research support: closed-loop water is becoming a product and service model

- VVater describes onsite reuse as customized, operated reuse systems that help facilities and communities address water scarcity through closed-loop service models.
- VVater also presents direct potable reuse as a way to purify wastewater into drinking-quality water while reducing dependence on conventional consumables.
- Implication for this book: greener living becomes normal when reuse, treatment, operation, and maintenance are made simple enough for real facilities to adopt.

Sources: VVater Onsite Reuse and Direct Potable Reuse pages.

Oil-derived and carbon-based products can help here when they are used responsibly. Permeable paving systems, membranes, liners, geotextiles, tanks, coatings, lightweight insulation, modular drainage systems, flexible pipes, and filtration components often rely on polymers and engineered carbon-based materials. The correct question is not whether those materials have a petroleum history. The correct question is whether they help cities retain water, reduce flooding, lower pumping energy, prevent contamination, extend asset life, and buy time for even greener materials to scale.

Engineer Hasna Ashur's smart-irrigation presentation adds another layer. Her cyber-agriculture concept uses root-zone data, artificial intelligence, and internet-of-things sensors so plants and soil conditions can guide irrigation before stress becomes visible. Hasna reports water-use-efficiency gains of up to 40 percent in pilot models. Whether a given deployment uses that exact result or a more modest number, the direction is clear: digital systems, sensors, polymer housings, tubes, valves, and water-delivery components can reduce waste today. The bridge to green is not only material substitution. It is smarter use of materials and water.

Jordan shows how water resilience becomes public finance

Engineer Hend El Fattah, a senior water and sanitation advisor in Jordan, explained why water resilience matters in a country with extremely low per-person water availability, heavy dependence on groundwater, irregular rainfall, refugee pressure, and growing flood risk. Her Amman case study described a flood-mitigation project using vegetated areas, drainage improvements, and an underground storage tank of about 2,500 cubic meters to capture, filter, slow, store, and reuse stormwater for urban vegetation and resilience.

That example belongs in this book because it shows that water infrastructure is not only environmental. It is financial. When flooding hits downtown markets, homes, roads, and public space, governments compensate, repair, and rebuild. When rainfall is captured and reused, the same water becomes a resilience asset. Carbon-based bridge materials can support those projects when they make storage, filtration, liners, pipes, permeable systems, and monitoring equipment cheaper, lighter, more durable, and easier to deploy.

Build back better means rebuilding systems, not repeating old patterns

Build-back-better models add a post-crisis lens. Dr. Etaz described recovery as a system problem, not merely a rebuilding problem, and warned that cities are not rebuilt by concrete alone; they are rebuilt by systems, trust, and coordination. That statement belongs in the heart of this book. If recovery simply replaces what was damaged with the same brittle materials and the same linear consumption model, it locks communities into the next disaster. If recovery uses bridge materials to build lower-loss systems, smarter water management, efficient buildings, and circular supply chains, the recovery becomes a transition.

Professor Doha, speaking on green urban innovation and resilient entrepreneurship in the Middle East and North Africa, added the finance layer. Her materials discussed post-conflict climate vulnerability, green reconstruction, climate hardware, green bonds, blended finance, local startups, and the danger of carbon lock-in. The most important lesson is not one exact number. It is the structure: reconstruction money can either recreate the emissions and waste profile of the past or finance a better industrial base for the future.

From green shocks to green shifts

Taken together, the GAoS distinguished guests' remarks point to a practical framework for the book: use today's established oil- and carbon-based material base to reduce waste now, but design every use as a bridge toward lower-carbon materials, circular systems, and greener everyday life. That means petroleum-derived materials should be judged by transition criteria. Do they extend the useful life of infrastructure? Do they reduce losses? Do they make buildings more efficient and healthier? Do they lower water stress? Do they support green jobs? Do they make resilience cheaper? Do they help new green materials enter the market by stabilizing the systems around them?

This approach is not dramatic, and that is why it can work. Most people were never asked whether they wanted an oil-based world; it simply became the normal way modern life worked. The greener future will become durable the same way: not by asking everyone to make heroic lifestyle changes every day, but by making better products, better streets, better buildings, better water systems, better training, and better incentives the default. At some point, green living should stop feeling like a separate identity. It should simply become the way we live.

Call to action: Choose one oil-derived or carbon-based material in your work and redesign its use as a bridge product. Ask how it can last longer, waste less, support green technology, and make the greener option easier for ordinary people to trust.

Epilogue - Transition, Stewardship, and the Future

The most credible path forward is not an overnight swap from one material world to another. It is a managed transition in which established oil- and carbon-based products are improved so they reduce leakage, corrosion, emissions, contamination, and waste while green materials and green manufacturing continue to gain trust, scale, and cost competitiveness.

That is the central argument of this book: use the established bridge responsibly. Improve what exists, reduce the harm built into current systems, and let those savings create the time, capital, and operating confidence required for greener materials to become standard without forcing society into brittle or unrealistic transitions.

If you have stayed with me this far, you already know I am not arguing for a miracle product or a one-step solution. I am arguing for leadership, design discipline, and the kind of operational honesty that turns a better idea into a standard people can live with.

There is a moment in every age when the old excuses begin to sound tired. Not false, exactly, but exhausted. Change takes time. The system is complicated. We need more study. We cannot move too fast. Each sentence contains some truth. Each can also become shelter when an industry no longer wants to confront the obvious.

The obvious, by now, should be impossible to miss. The world is too expensive to keep wasting what it already has, too politically brittle to normalize preventable failure, and too environmentally strained to treat leakage as routine. That threshold - between tolerated waste and disciplined stewardship - is where I have tried to stay.

The future will not arrive as spectacle. It will arrive as standard. It will be visible in specifications, training manuals, maintenance windows, monitoring dashboards, procurement language, and changed expectations inside crews, utilities, and cities. That is how big systems actually change.

That is why I have used oil as a doorway rather than a destination. The real issue is whether the systems that still rely on oil-derived materials, fluid transport, and long-lived infrastructure can become more accountable, more repairable, and less wasteful than the systems they replace.

The future that deserves to survive will leak less, test more intelligently, train more seriously, and honor labor by asking it to do higher-value work. It will treat proof as a form of public trust. It will understand that affordability is built as much in the trench as it is in the market. It will stop confusing preventable weakness with inevitability.

The next standard begins before the next crisis

I do not expect the world to adopt this argument because it is elegant. I expect it to move only when enough owners, workers, and communities conclude that the old way is no longer affordable. That is why I have written this book as both a case for infrastructure and a case against delay. The point is not to wait for the next San Bruno, the next Merrimack Valley, the next citywide outage, the next saltwater emergency, or the next snow-drought shock. The point is to build the standard before the next crisis makes the cost of not building it impossible to ignore.

What I want us to remember

That, to me, is what the fight has always been about. Not novelty for its own sake. Not nostalgia for old energy. But a determination to stop wasting so much of what we have already worked so hard to move.

Why this stays personal for me

I come back to Costa Rica here because it is where the problem first acquired faces for me. I remember rough roads, mud, remote houses, church visits with my father, and the way basic services could never be taken for granted. In some places, water pressure was inconsistent, humidity lived inside the walls, and a clean, dry home was not an assumption but an achievement. I also remember the people who formed me and this book is my way to honor their life work and efforts towards a cleaner world and creating a supporting environment for future intellectual and materials development.

My challenge to you

So this is my challenge to you. Look harder at what you buy, what you approve, what you normalize, and what you ignore. If you lead a city, a utility, an engineering firm, a health system, a foundation, or a fund, ask what cleaner, safer, expandable infrastructure would unlock if it became standard price instead of premium price.

Support the technologies, purchasing decisions, procurement standards, and public leaders that move in that direction. Challenge institutions, yes, but challenge yourself first. The status quo survives because it is familiar. Real change begins when we decide that familiarity is no longer a good enough reason to keep paying for preventable weakness.

What I believe becomes possible next

When I say this is not a quick fix, I mean that every replacement decision should be treated as a generational choice. A trusted segment is a segment we do not have to revisit. That confidence scales. It lets communities stop spending tomorrow's budget repairing yesterday's uncertainty and start building new markets, cleaner supply systems, and stronger forms of human settlement instead.

When I imagine future generations, I do not only imagine cleaner cities. I imagine children inheriting rivers that were not sacrificed to avoidable leaks, forests supported by better water movement, coastal communities protected by smarter conveyance, underwater laboratories that teach us how to live carefully in closed systems, and off-world habitats where purity, pressure, and continuity are treated with the seriousness they deserve.

That is the hopeful version of this book. Not that oil saves us by being burned without thought. But that oil, used rightly, helps us build the disciplined infrastructure that lets humanity survive, expand, and thrive without wasting the only world we have—or the next environments we may someday enter.

References

EPA. Summary of the Clean Water Act. U.S. Environmental Protection Agency. https://www.epa.gov/laws-regulations/summary-clean-water-act

EPA. Benefits of Trees and Vegetation. U.S. Environmental Protection Agency. https://www.epa.gov/heatislands/benefits-trees-and-vegetation

EPA. Using Trees and Vegetation to Reduce Heat Islands. U.S. Environmental Protection Agency. https://www.epa.gov/heatislands/using-trees-and-vegetation-reduce-heat-islands

NASA Earth Observatory / NASA Science. Mapping the Amazon; Tropical Deforestation; Amazon deforestation and climate materials. https://science.nasa.gov/earth/

NOAA. International Section - Submarine Cables. https://www.noaa.gov/submarine-cables

HEET. Gas Leaks Map. https://www.heet.org/gas-leaks-map

HEET. New Maps: Gas Leaks & Plans for New Gas Pipes in MA. https://www.heet.org/blog-items/new-maps-gas-leaks-plans-for-new-gas-pipes-in-ma

MWRA. Massachusetts Water Resources Authority. https://www.mwra.com

NEWIN / NEEFC. Water infrastructure resources and New England Water Innovation Network materials. https://neefc.org/water-infrastructure/

NECEC. New England Clean Energy Connect. https://www.necleanenergyconnect.org

Greentown Labs. https://greentownlabs.com

MassCEC. Massachusetts Clean Energy Center. https://www.masscec.com

CEBA. Clean Energy Buyers Association. https://ceba.org

David Gardiner and Associates. Building infrastructure and trust role of CBAs. https://www.dgardiner.com/building-infrastructure-and-trust-role-cbas/

CABA. California Advanced Biofuels Alliance. https://www.caadvancedbiofuelsalliance.org

CleanTech Open. https://www.cleantechopen.org

WinnCompanies / Winn Green sustainability materials. https://www.winncompanies.com

Femern A/S. Fehmarnbelt immersed tunnel project materials. https://femern.com

FAO / African Union / Great Green Wall restoration materials. https://www.fao.org

U.S. Department of Energy. Methane Mitigation Technologies Multi-Year Program Plan. https://www.energy.gov/sites/default/files/2025-01/Methane%20Mitigation%20Technologies%20Multi-Year%20Program%20Plan_0.pdf

User-provided investor deck (legacy company materials).

User-provided 2015 technical deck (legacy company materials).

European Commission. Speech by President von der Leyen at the Summit on the Future of Energy Security. 24 April 2025. https://ec.europa.eu/commission/presscorner/api/files/document/print/en/speech_25_1100/SPEECH_25_1100_EN.pdf

European Commission. Opening address by President von der Leyen on the Clean Industrial Deal. 26 February 2025. https://ec.europa.eu/commission/presscorner/api/files/document/print/en/speech_25_628/SPEECH_25_628_EN.pdf

UK Government. PM remarks at the IEA Future of Energy Security summit. 24 April 2025. https://www.gov.uk/government/speeches/pm-remarks-at-the-iea-future-of-energy-security-summit-24-april-2025

UK Government. Prime Minister Rishi Sunak's article in the Telegraph. 12 March 2024. https://www.gov.uk/government/speeches/prime-minister-rishi-sunaks-article-in-the-telegraph-12-march-2024

United Nations. Secretary-General's remarks at the United Nations Water Conference. 22 March 2023. https://www.un.org/sg/en/content/sg/speeches/2023-03-22/secretary-generals-remarks-the-united-nations-water-conference

United Nations Sustainable Development Group. Secretary-General's remarks to the Opening of the High-level Special Event on Climate Action. 2025. https://unsdg.un.org/latest/announcements/un-secretary-generals-remarks-opening-high-level-special-event-climate-action

Government of Brazil. President Lula's speech at the session on energy transition at the Leaders' Summit of COP30. 7 November 2025. https://www.gov.br/planalto/en/follow-the-government/speeches-statements/2025/11/president-lula2019s-speech-at-the-session-on-energy-transition-at-the-leaders2019-summit-of-cop30

Government of Brazil. President Lula's Speech at the Session 'Climate and Nature: Forests and Oceans' during the COP30 Leaders' Summit. 6 November 2025. https://www.gov.br/planalto/en/follow-the-government/speeches-statements/2025/11/president-lula2019s-speech-at-the-session-201cclimate-and-nature-forests-and-oceans201d-during-the-cop30-leaders2019-summit

United Nations General Debate. Barbados statement by Prime Minister Mia Amor Mottley. 26 September 2025. https://gadebate.un.org/en/80/barbados

UN DESA. Statement by Carlos Alvarado Quesada, President of Costa Rica, General Debate 75th Session. https://sdgs.un.org/ga75-statement/costarica

Prime Minister of India. PM's remarks at India Energy Week 2025. 11 February 2025. https://www.pmindia.gov.in/en/news_updates/pms-remarks-at-india-energy-week-2025/

Prime Minister of India. PM Sets Ambitious Vision for India's Future in 78th Independence Day Address. 15 August 2024. https://www.pmindia.gov.in/en/news_updates/pm-sets-ambitious-vision-for-indias-future-in-78th-independence-day-address/

The Official Website of the President of the Republic of Kenya. Kenya is committed to clean energy. 2 March 2023. https://www.president.go.ke/kenya-is-committed-to-clean-energy/

The Official Website of the President of the Republic of Kenya. President Ruto: Innovation is the answer to unemployment. 6 December 2022. https://www.president.go.ke/president-ruto-innovation-is-the-answer-to-unemployment/

Élysée. Speech by the President of the French Republic at the Conference of Ambassadors. 1 September 2022. https://www.elysee.fr/en/emmanuel-macron/2022/09/01/speech-by-the-president-of-the-french-republic-at-the-conference-of-ambassadors-1

PHMSA. National Pipeline Performance Measures. U.S. Department of Transportation. https://www.phmsa.dot.gov/data-and-statistics/pipeline/national-pipeline-performance-measures

PHMSA. Distribution, Transmission & Gathering, LNG, and Liquid Accident and Incident Data. https://www.phmsa.dot.gov/data-and-statistics/pipeline/distribution-transmission-gathering-lng-and-liquid-accident-and-incident-data

U.S. Department of Transportation / PHMSA. Pipeline Safety R&D Updated Plan (incident summaries). https://www.phmsa.dot.gov/sites/phmsa.dot.gov/files/2023-04/Report%20to%20Congress%20-%20PHMSA%20FY2021-22%20Pipeline%20Safety%20R%26D%20Update%20Plan.pdf

NTSB. Pacific Gas and Electric Company Natural Gas Transmission Pipeline Rupture and Fire, San Bruno, California. https://www.ntsb.gov/investigations/AccidentReports/Reports/PAR1101.pdf

California Public Utilities Commission. San Bruno Incident summary. https://www.cpuc.ca.gov/regulatory-services/safety/gas-safety-and-reliability-branch/san-bruno-incident

NTSB. Natural Gas-Fueled Building Explosion and Resulting Fire, East Harlem, New York. https://www.ntsb.gov/investigations/AccidentReports/Reports/PAR1501.pdf

NTSB. Overpressurization of Natural Gas Distribution System, Explosions, and Fires, Merrimack Valley, Massachusetts. https://www.ntsb.gov/investigations/AccidentReports/Reports/PAR1902.pdf

Massachusetts Department of Public Utilities. Settlement related to Columbia Gas and Merrimack Valley gas explosions. https://www.mass.gov/news/department-of-public-utilities-approves-settlement-related-to-columbia-gass-role-in-merrimack-valley-gas-explosions

WSSC Water. Water Main Breaks. https://www.wsscwater.com/what-we-do/major-projects/pipes-and-infrastructure-improvements-and-maintenance/water-main-breaks

Rajani, B. et al. Empirical analysis of large diameter water main break consequences. https://www.sciencedirect.com/science/article/pii/S0921344916300490

U.S. Geological Survey. Approximate inland extent of saltwater intrusion at the base of the Biscayne aquifer, Miami-Dade County, Florida, 2022. https://www.usgs.gov/maps/approximate-inland-extent-saltwater-intrusion-base-biscayne-aquifer-miami-dade-county-florida

U.S. Geological Survey. Origins and delineation of saltwater intrusion in the Biscayne aquifer and changes in the distribution of saltwater in Miami-Dade County, Florida. https://pubs.usgs.gov/publication/sir20145025

City of Miami. King Tides. https://www.miami.gov/My-Government/Climate-Change-in-the-City-of-Miami/King-Tides

City of Miami. Sea level rise stormwater management information. https://www.miami.gov/My-Government/Departments/Office-of-Capital-Improvements/SWMP-Sea-Level-Rise-Info

Miami-Dade County. Septic System Care. https://www.miamidade.gov/global/environment/ecosystems/septic-system-care.page

Miami-Dade County. Water Quality Protection. https://wwwx.miamidade.gov/environment/water-protection.asp

NOAA NCCOS. Model identifies septic system discharge hotspots in southeast Florida. https://coastalscience.noaa.gov/news/model-identifies-septic-system-discharge-hotspots-in-southeast-florida/

NOAA / NIDIS. Snow Drought Current Conditions and Impacts in the West (March 2026). https://www.drought.gov/drought-status-updates/snow-drought-current-conditions-and-impacts-west-2026-03-12

Climate Central. Record Snow Drought Limits Western Water Supplies. https://www.climatecentral.org/climate-matters/western-snowpack-drought-2026

NASA Earth Observatory. The West Faces Snow Drought. https://science.nasa.gov/earth/earth-observatory/the-west-faces-snow-drought/

California Department of Water Resources. February storms provide a much-needed boost but statewide snowpack remains below average. https://water.ca.gov/News/News-

Releases/2026/Feb-2026/February-Storms-Provide-a-Much-Needed-Boost-but-Statewide-Snowpack-Remains-Below-Average

California Department of Water Resources. Delta Conveyance. https://water.ca.gov/Programs/State-Water-Project/Delta-Conveyance

California Department of Water Resources. Department of Water Resources Approves Delta Conveyance Project. https://water.ca.gov/News/News-Releases/2023/Dec-23/Department-of-Water-Resources-Approves-Delta-Conveyance-Project

U.S. Bureau of Reclamation. Colorado River Basin Post-2026 Operations. https://www.usbr.gov/ColoradoRiverBasin/post2026

U.S. Bureau of Reclamation. Interior secures 18 short-term agreements to boost Colorado River conservation. https://www.usbr.gov/newsroom/news-release/5148

Congressional Research Service. Management of the Colorado River: Water Allocations, Drought, and the Federal Role. https://www.congress.gov/crs-product/R45546

PPI Municipal & Industrial Division. High-performance HDPE for water piping systems. https://conduitcalc.plasticpipe.org/municipal_pipe/

PPI. Handbook of PE Pipe / PE Handbook. https://www.plasticpipe.org/PPI-Home/Shared_Content/Shop/PE-Handbook.aspx

Author-supplied SolidMelt development plan, especially pages 44-45 on pricing and cost of ownership.

WSSC Water. WSSC Water is Winter Ready. https://www.wsscwater.com/customer-service/customer-service-faq/wssc-winter-ready

California Department of Water Resources. DWR is Taking Action as High Temperatures Prompt Early Snow Runoff. https://water.ca.gov/News/Blog/2026/Mar-2026/DWR-is-Taking-Action-as-High-Temperatures-Prompt-Early-Snow-Runoff

Miami-Dade County. Saltwater Intrusion. https://www.miamidade.gov/global/water/conservation/saltwater-intrusion.page

NTSB. Overpressurized Gas Distribution System Caused Explosions, Fires. https://www.ntsb.gov/news/press-releases/Pages/NR20190924.aspx

MTA. Heavy rain and other flood events: service guide. https://www.mta.info/guides/weather-service-guide/storm-flood-hurricane-service

MTA. MTA Announces Completion of Sandy Resiliency Work in F Line's East River Tunnel. https://www.mta.info/press-release/mta-announces-completion-of-sandy-resiliency-work-f-lines-east-river-tunnel

New York City Department of Environmental Protection. Flooding and Climate Change. https://www.nyc.gov/site/dep/environment/flood-prevention.page

New York City Department of Environmental Protection. Combined Sewer Overflows. https://home4.nyc.gov/site/dep/water/combined-sewer-overflows.page

City of Boston. Climate Resilience / Flooding Boston. https://www.boston.gov/so/departments/environment/flooding-boston

City of Boston. Climate protection for vulnerable MBTA stations (GO Boston 2030 / Climate Ready Boston material). https://www.boston.gov/sites/default/files/document-file-06-2019/climate_protection_for_vulnerable_mbta_stations.pdf

Boston Water and Sewer Commission. Combined Sewer Overflows. https://www.bwsc.org/environment-education/water-sewer-and-stormwater/cso-public-notification

EPA. Drinking Water Distribution Systems. https://www.epa.gov/dwsixyearreview/drinking-water-distribution-systems

EPA. Drinking Water Distribution System Tools and Resources. https://www.epa.gov/dwreginfo/drinking-water-distribution-system-tools-and-resources

EPA Region 8. Loss of Pressure in Drinking Water Systems in Wyoming and on Tribal Lands in EPA Region 8. https://www.epa.gov/region8-waterops/loss-pressure-drinking-water-systems-wyoming-and-tribal-lands-epa-region-8

EPA. Managing Contaminated Drinking Water Post-Hurricane. https://www.epa.gov/emergency-response-research/managing-contaminated-drinking-water-post-hurricane

PPI. Potable Water Benefits - HDPE Pipe. https://www.plasticpipe.org/MunicipalIndustrial/Municipal_Industrial/Applications/Potable-Water-Benefits---HDPE.aspx

EPA. EPA's Response Letter to AGA Regarding MDPE and HDPE as a Non-Porous Surface. https://www.epa.gov/pcbs/epas-response-letter-aga-regarding-mdpe-and-hdpe-non-porous-surface

Cornell Legal Information Institute. 49 CFR § 192.281 Plastic pipe. https://www.law.cornell.edu/cfr/text/49/192.281

Williams JD, Romo T, Sclafani AP, Cho H. Porous high-density polyethylene implants in auricular reconstruction. PubMed. https://pubmed.ncbi.nlm.nih.gov/9193216/

Ali K, Mohan A, Liu T, et al. Total Ear Reconstruction Using Porous Polyethylene. PubMed Central. https://pmc.ncbi.nlm.nih.gov/articles/PMC5550314/

Perozzo FAG, Ku YC, Kshettry V, et al. High-Density Porous Polyethylene Implant Cranioplasty: A Systematic Review of Outcomes. PubMed. https://pubmed.ncbi.nlm.nih.gov/38682928/

Additional official sources incorporated in this budget and affordability update:

- U.S. Environmental Protection Agency. EPA's 7th Drinking Water Infrastructure Needs Survey and Assessment. 2025 update.
- U.S. Environmental Protection Agency. Clean Watersheds Needs Survey: 2022 Results and Report to Congress.
- U.S. Environmental Protection Agency. Water Affordability Needs Assessment. 2024.
- U.S. Bureau of Labor Statistics. Consumer Price Index, Table 2, February 2026 detailed expenditure categories.
- U.S. Energy Information Administration. Electric Power Annual, Table 2.4, average price of electricity to ultimate customers, 2014-2024.
- U.S. Energy Information Administration. Natural Gas Annual, Table 1 and Table 23, average residential natural gas price, 2020-2024.
- New York City Water Board. FY2026 Adopted Budget and Rate History.
- Massachusetts Water Resources Authority. Water & Sewer Rates and FY2026 Final Budget projections through FY2030.
- Boston Water and Sewer Commission. 2025 Proposed Rate Document and 2026 Final Rate Document.
- WSSC Water. FY2026 budget approval materials; winter readiness and break-and-leak repair cost reports; cost-of-service study.
- Miami-Dade Water and Sewer Department. Capital Improvement Program and FY23-24 investment update.
- City of Miami Beach. Utility Rate Structures for fiscal year 2025/2026.
- Philadelphia Water Department. 2025 rate request and bill impact statement.
- Los Angeles Department of Water and Power. FY2025-2026 Water Revenue Fund final budget.
- National Grid. 2025 Upstate New York Rate Plan approved highlights.
- Con Edison. Gas safety and climate / leak-prone pipe replacement materials, 2024-2025.
- U.S. Department of Energy. Low-Income Energy Affordability Data (LEAD) Tool, energy-burden definition.
- Administration for Children and Families. Low Income Household Water Assistance Program materials and milestones.

NOAA National Ocean Service. Final Programmatic Environmental Impact Statement for Surveying and Mapping Projects in U.S. Waters for Coastal and Marine Data Acquisition. Submarine cables carrying about 99 percent of international communications traffic. https://cdn.oceanservice.noaa.gov/oceanserviceprod/about/environmental-compliance/final-peis/Chapter%204%20Cumulative%20Impacts.pdf

Florida International University. About FIU Aquarius. https://environment.fiu.edu/aquarius/about/

NASA. About NEEMO (NASA Extreme Environment Mission Operations). https://www.nasa.gov/missions/analog-field-testing/neemo/about-neemo-nasa-extreme-environment-mission-operations/

U.S. Government Accountability Office. Offshore Oil and Gas: Updated Regulations Needed to Improve Pipeline Oversight and Decommissioning (GAO-21-293). https://www.gao.gov/products/gao-21-293

NASA Johnson Space Center. Life Support Subsystems. https://www.nasa.gov/reference/jsc-life-support-subsystems/

NASA. Crew Systems / Orion Environmental Control and Life Support Systems. https://www.nasa.gov/reference/crew-systems/

NASA. NASA Achieves Water Recovery Milestone on International Space Station. https://www.nasa.gov/missions/station/iss-research/nasa-achieves-water-recovery-milestone-on-international-space-station/

NASA. Lunar South Pole Oxygen Pipeline. https://www.nasa.gov/general/lunar-south-pole-oxygen-pipeline/

NASA. Cryogenic Fluid Management. https://www.nasa.gov/space-technology-mission-directorate/tdm/cryogenic-fluid-management-cfm/

Canada Energy Regulator. Indigenous Monitoring. https://www.cer-rec.gc.ca/en/consultation-engagement/indigenous-engagement/indigenous-monitoring.html

State of Michigan, Department of Environment, Great Lakes, and Energy. Line 5 overview. https://www.michigan.gov/egle/about/featured/line5/overview

Earthjustice. Standing Rock Sioux Tribe Takes Action to Protect Culture and Environment from Massive Crude Oil Pipeline. https://earthjustice.org/press/2016/standing-rock-sioux-tribe-takes-action-to-protect-culture-and-environment-from-massive-crude-oil-pipeline

UNICEF Data. Access to drinking water / Progress on Household Drinking Water and Sanitation 2000–2024. https://data.unicef.org/resources/wash-water-supply-sanitation-hygiene/

UNESCO. Global water crisis aggravated by gender inequalities according to new UN Report; UN World Water Development Report 2026. https://www.unesco.org/en/articles/global-water-crisis-aggravated-gender-inequalities-according-new-un-report and https://www.unesco.org/en/world-water-report-2026?hub=68313

Gates Foundation. Water, Sanitation & Hygiene strategy and innovation materials. https://www.gatesfoundation.org/our-work/programs/global-growth-and-opportunity/water-sanitation-and-hygiene

World Vision Evidence. The role of piped-water supplies in advancing health, economic development, and gender equality in rural communities. https://evidence.worldvision.org/research-and-resources/the-role-of-piped-water-supplies-in-advancing-health-economic-development-and-gender-equality-in-rural-communities/

World Bank. Karnataka Sustainable Rural Water Supply Program. https://www.worldbank.org/en/news/press-release/2023/03/28/world-bank-approves-363-million-to-improve-water-supply-to-2-million-rural-households-in-the-indian-state-of-karnataka

World Bank. Bangladesh Rural Water, Sanitation and Hygiene for Human Capital Development Project. https://www.worldbank.org/en/news/press-release/2020/09/25/world-bank-helps-bangladesh-ensure-safe-water-and-sanitation-in-rural-areas

World Bank. Strengthening Water Resilience in Ethiopia's Rural Communities. https://www.worldbank.org/en/news/feature/2025/05/22/strengthening-water-resilience-in-ethiopia-s-rural-communities-afe

World Bank. Improving the Rural Water and Sanitation Information Systems in Latin America and the Caribbean Region (SIASAR). https://www.worldbank.org/en/results/2017/04/04/improving-rural-water-sanitation-information-systems-latinamerica

FAO. Solar-powered Irrigation and On-Farm Production; Positive prospects for solar-powered irrigation systems. https://www.fao.org/land-water/overview/onehealth/solar/en/ and https://www.fao.org/newsroom/detail/Positive-prospects-for-solar-powered-irrigation-systems/es

CarbonCure Technologies. Technologies and About pages. https://www.carboncure.com/technologies/ and https://www.carboncure.com/about/

UNICEF. Handwashing; Hygiene; WASH overview. https://www.unicef.org/wash/handwashing, https://www.unicef.org/wash/hygiene, and https://www.unicef.org/wash

WHO. Water, Sanitation and Hygiene (WASH) overview; WASH and IPC in health emergencies. https://www.who.int/health-topics/water-sanitation-and-hygiene-wash and https://www.who.int/emergencies/operations/ipc-wash

WHO and UNICEF. Progress on WASH in health care facilities 2000–2021 and related press materials. https://www.who.int/publications/i/item/9789240058699 and https://www.unicef.org/press-releases/half-health-care-facilities-globally-lack-basic-hygiene-services-who-unicef

WHO, UNICEF, Gavi, and Gates Foundation. Global immunization efforts have saved at least 154 million lives over the past 50 years. https://www.unicef.org/tajikistan/press-releases/global-immunization-efforts-have-saved-least-154-million-lives-over-past-50-years

Global Ambassadors of Sustainability (GAoS). About us. https://www.gaos.earth/

GAoS / U.S. Green Chamber of Commerce. GGSL Academy. https://www.gaos.earth/index.php/ggsl-academy/

GAoS and Global Green Chamber of Commerce. International Committee of Social Entrepreneurship & Sustainability (ICSES). https://www.gaos.earth/index.php/icses/

GAoS. International Committee on Public Policy, Diplomacy, and Sustainability (ICPDS). https://www.gaos.earth/index.php/working-groups/

Global Ambassadors of Sustainability. LinkedIn company page. https://ca.linkedin.com/company/global-ambassadors-of-sustainability

GAoS live session recording. YouTube. https://www.youtube.com/live/Qq_-Vd449oY

GAoS live session recording. YouTube. https://www.youtube.com/live/npJ5tJvEdR4

GAoS live session recording. YouTube. https://www.youtube.com/live/zLmsq77SOXU

GAoS live session recording. YouTube. https://www.youtube.com/live/wFXoytOOZ_4

GAoS live session recording. YouTube. https://www.youtube.com/live/I5sDw_erePU

GAoS live session recording. YouTube. https://www.youtube.com/live/zZwhmC5tPZM

Amigo Energy. Fossil fuels overview. https://amigoenergy.com/blog/fossil-fuels/

Mobasser, Shariat, PhD. Balancing the essential role of carbon-based materials. LinkedIn. https://www.linkedin.com/pulse/balancing-essential-role-carbon-based-materials-shariat-mobasser-phd-yedhe/

www.ingramcontent.com/pod-product-compliance
Lightning Source LLC
LaVergne TN
LVHW010615110826
845149LV00003B/926
* 9 7 9 8 9 9 5 0 1 8 8 4 1 *